Other titles by Weldon Kees
available from the University of Nebraska Press

The Collected Poems of Weldon Kees (Revised Edition)
Donald Justice, ed.

Weldon Kees and the Midcentury Generation
Letters, 1935–1955
Robert E. Knoll, ed.

SELECTED SHORT STORIES OF

WELDON KEES

Edited and with an introduction by
DANA GIOIA

UNIVERSITY OF NEBRASKA PRESS
LINCOLN AND LONDON

CONTENTS

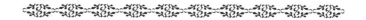

INTRODUCTION

WHEN WELDON KEES published his first book of verse in 1941, he was probably better known as a short story writer than a poet. There were only thirty-nine poems in *The Last Man*, a book which contained virtually every poem he had published up to that time, while there were about forty of his short stories in print in various magazines and journals. Two of his stories, "I Should Worry" and "The Evening of the Fourth of July," had recently appeared in the prestigious *New Directions* annuals, and nine others had been published in *Prairie Schooner,* one of the most influential small magazines of the period, whose editor, Lowry Charles Wimberly, championed Kees's work. Likewise his stories had been nominated almost every year for a decade in the popular annual anthology *Best Short Stories,* where in 1941 its editor, Edward J. O'Brien, had reprinted Kees's "The Life of the Mind" and had dedicated the volume to him. At the age of twenty-nine, Kees seemed on the brink of an important career in fiction. With a book of poems just out, could a volume of short stories be far behind? Or even a novel? In one contributor's note, it was announced that Kees had signed a contract with Alfred Knopf for a novel (the still unpublished *Fall Quarter*). But Kees never published a novel with Knopf or any other firm, and no volume of short stories was ever forthcoming. In 1945 two more stories appeared in college magazines, and then after nearly fifteen years of steady production, Kees simply stopped writing fiction.

It is not unusual for an American poet to be equally interested in writing short fiction. As our first great master of
both forms, Edgar Allan Poe, demonstrated, the techniques
of lyric poetry and the short story have much in common,
and many subsequent writers excelled at both, among them
Stephen Crane, Conrad Aiken, William Carlos Williams,
Robert Penn Warren, and Delmore Schwartz. Like them,
Kees worked comfortably in either genre. What is unusual, if
not unparalleled, about Kees's case, is that he put so much
energy into his fiction, enjoyed some degree of success, and
then suddenly abandoned the form he worked so long to
master.

Someday a biographer may satisfactorily explain why Kees
turned away from fiction. It seems difficult to believe that he
was completely dissatisfied with everything he had written.
Although he had published many undistinguished stories, he
had also written at least half a dozen first-rate pieces, and his
command of the form was getting stronger each year. The
later pieces had just the flexibility of tone and breadth of
imagination the earlier work lacked. Perhaps there were
personal reasons why Kees abandoned fiction at the age of
thirty-one. Had he gradually come to the conclusion that his
talents could be better realized in some other medium? Most
likely he simply became too busy with other projects to continue writing fiction.

In 1943 at just about the point when he stopped writing
stories, Kees moved from Denver to New York where he
embarked on a succession of jobs all more engrossing than
his position as a research librarian in Denver. First came his
spot on *Time*'s editorial staff where he wrote on films, books,
and music. Then came a position as a screenwriter for Para-
mount newsreel, and eventually a post as art editor of *The
Nation*. Kees also began painting seriously and took an active
part in the avant-garde gallery scene. He continued writing

poetry, but now published it mainly in East Coast magazines. More importantly, Kees also began reviewing on a regular basis. He wrote about everything, at least everything artistic, from jazz to movies, from abstract art to modern poetry. While his reviews from the 'thirties had appeared in smaller magazines, usually in the Midwest, his pieces now began appearing regularly in the most influential journals of the period, including *The Nation, The New Republic, Partisan Review,* and *The New York Times.* Reviewing often builds a writer's reputation more quickly and dependably than publishing poems or short stories, and Kees's aggressive, witty style earned him more attention and broader recognition than he had received for his original work. While many of the assignments were hackwork, they were gratifying hackwork, and Kees obviously poured a great deal of talent and energy into each one. Many young writers abandon the uncertain travail of creative work for the dependable and sometimes lucrative pleasures of reviewing, so it is scarcely amazing that Kees abandoned fiction. The remarkable thing is that he found time to continue writing poetry.

II.

Whatever the reasons Kees abandoned fiction, it is important to remember three facts while reading his short stories. First, his fiction came early in his relatively brief career. All of the stories in this selection were written by the time he was thirty. Second, most of his stories reflect his regional background as a Midwesterner. With only two exceptions, all of Kees's forty-three short stories and sketches were written before he moved to New York, and many of them present specifically Nebraskan themes. Finally, the short stories represent a major part of his literary work. Although they are almost unknown today, they make up the bulk of his published work and are the products of the time when he took his fiction as seriously as his poetry.

Each of these points requires some elaboration. First, Kees's short stories are early work – not juvenilia but the work of a young writer testing the limits of his imagination. Kees's literary career spans just over twenty years – from the time he published his first mature stories at twenty until his disappearance at forty-one. His published fiction all appeared in the first half of his career, and so it provides the most comprehensive record available of his early development as a writer. The importance of this work is stengthened by its distinctiveness. From his earliest published work, Kees had an amazing command of literary technique as well as a frightening clarity of personal vision. Almost every story or poem, no matter how early, sounds like nobody else but Kees. His work may have grown deeper and more complex as he got older, but it never changed.

Kees's short stories also have a regional character almost entirely absent from his poetry. His fiction deals with the world of his childhood and adolescence – the Midwest. Almost half of his early stories take place in Weston, Nebraska, an imaginary town he peopled with recurrent characters. The deliberate creation of Weston suggests that at some point Kees planned a volume of interconnected stories. His model was almost certainly Sherwood Anderson's *Winesburg, Ohio*, which enjoyed a classic position in American literature in the 'twenties and 'thirties. Hemingway, Wolfe, Faulkner, Steinbeck, Saroyan, and Caldwell all used Anderson as a model; so it is not surprising that Kees, who came out of the same American heartland, would also turn to him. Kees was also influenced in his creation of Weston by several other "regional" works, most notably Edgar Lee Masters' *Spoon River Anthology* (Anderson's own inspiration for the Winesburg tales) and Edwin Arlington Robinson's bleak poems of Tilbury Town. Kees tailored the conventions of regional literature to suit his own needs. Never a naturalist by sympathy, he followed Anderson in using documentary techniques to convey a highly personal vision.

Finally it is necessary to remember that Kees's short stories are a major part of his literary work. This is not to say that his fiction is ultimately as important as his poetry, but rather that it is impossible to judge Kees's achievement as a writer without knowing his short stories. Although both the fiction and the poetry can be read independently with satisfaction, when read together they add resonance to one another. Twenty years ago in his valuable introduction to *The Collected Poems,* Donald Justice said, "The poetry of Kees makes its deepest impression when read as a body of work rather than a collection of isolated moments of brilliance." This same insight must be extended to Kees's total literary oeuvre, poetry and prose alike.

Kees knew how easily an artist could be labeled a dilettante for working in more than one medium. As a professional poet, short story writer, journalist, musician, painter, photographer, and filmmaker, he had often experienced the indifference or condescension of critics who believed no one could do serious work in more than one art form. One month before his disappearance, Kees discussed this problem obliquely in a review (*The New Republic,* June 20, 1955) of Vernon Duke's marvellous but now forgotten memoir, *Passport to Paris.* Duke, who had worked successfully both as a popular song writer and a serious composer, complained that this musical ambidexterity had actually worked against him. Kees quoted approvingly Duke's claim that his versatility "has in reality been infuriating to most musical people. Just why that is I have no way of knowing, but the critical boys seem to think there is something monstrous and unnatural about a composer writing two different kinds of music."

III.

Poetry and prose are also two different kinds of music, and the first thing one notices when reading Kees's short stories is how different they are from his poems. This difference is most noticeable in the style, especially in the diction and syntax. Compare for example, two passages written about the same time, one in prose, the other in verse. First, here is the opening of "I Should Worry," one of his finest stories:

> *Arch Boyle lounged in a broken wicker chair in front of his used auto parts place. A half-smoked cigarette was pasted in one corner of his mouth, and from the other corner a broken toothpick hung. Across the street, in front of the City Mission, an old man was sweeping the sidewalk with a worn broom. A bunch of kids were rollerskating, and each time they went by, the old man had to stop sweeping, leaning on his broom until they passed. The wheels of their skates rasped on the concrete, and whenever they rolled over divisions in the sidewalk, they made a clacking sound like a needle on a cracked Victrola record. The old man would watch them and then return to his work, raising a thin sift of dust.*

Kees's prose is deliberately flat. He describes the scene around Arch Boyle's auto parts store matter-of-factly in a tone as neutral and seemingly objective as a black-and-white photograph. Words seem chosen for their meaning, not their sound. They are strictly denotative, connotative of nothing but the boredom of everyday life. The diction is extremely sparse, with few polysyllabic or Latinate words. The vocabulary is so limited that once a word is introduced it is often used again, as if even in the opening paragraph Kees wanted to restrict the number of sounds and images. The syntax is smooth and unexceptional. The sentences are relatively short and straightforward. Everything in this passage is controlled to focus the reader's attention on the scene itself and not the description of it.

Compare this to the opening stanza of the poem, "To a Contemporary":

> *Memories rich as Proust's or Baudelaire's are yours,*
> *You think: snarled ravelings of doubt at evening; scents*
> *Of women, dazed with pleasure, whose white legs and arms*
> *Once coiled with languor around you; arguments*
> *With undistinguished friends, their bigotries each year*
> *More fixed. Lamps in the mist that light strange faces fill*
> *Your nights; your fingers drum upon the table as you stare,*
> *Uncertain, at the floor. Un vieux boudoir? Impossible!*
> *You frequently compare yourself to those whose memories*
> *Are cruel, contemptible, like naked bone.*

The verse passage is, of course, very different. Here the language is luxurious, even excessive. Whereas the prose passage pretended to be impersonal, the poem announces itself at once as deeply emotional and subjective. It also opens with allusions to Proust and Baudelaire, a gesture which would have been unthinkable in the unintellectual style of the story, and then proceeds with a frenetic catalogue of images. Whereas the prose focused sharply on one, slow everyday scene like the fixed camera in an Italian neo-realist film, the poem cuts so quickly from one scene to another that it is sometimes hard to know exactly where one is. Likewise the prose narrative concentrates almost exclusively on the sense of sight with only the monotonous sound of the rollerskates in the background, whereas the poem specifically addresses itself to the senses of smell, touch, sight, and sound as well as to the interior senses of imagination and memory, so absent from the prose which dwelt purposely only on the exterior of things.

The diction of the poem is also more extravagant than any-thing in the story. From the very first word the language is heavily Latinate, but the words are used so forcefully and with such cosmopolitan *sangfroid* that they slip by almost unnoticed. The syntax is also very complex with one phrase piled on another in strange appositions. Noteworthy too are the strong enjambments in almost every line where phrases are broken up between lines ("their bigotries each year / more fixed," "fill / your nights," "those whose memories / are cruel"). This device forces the reader again and again to recognize that this impassioned speech is an artifact, a piece of verse, that the language, which seems so violent and spon-taneous, is in reality metrical and controlled. And if the reader stops to look at the stanza, he will discover that its form is allusive and foreign – loose but elaborately rhymed alexandrines – a measure borrowed from Baudelaire. How different this is from the prose style which calls so little at-tention to itself.

For Kees then prose was clearly a different medium than verse, and so it is not surprising that he used the short story for different effects than he did his poetry. Kees's verse tends to be forceful and confident. His poems, even the quiet ones, move quickly towards a powerful climax, as one image tumbles kaleidoscopically into the next until suddenly one discovers the kaleidoscope has become a maelstrom. His stories, in contrast, are quiet and intensely focused. They achieve their savage effects in a cold, methodical way. Not only do they move slowly, sometimes they never seem to move at all but remain fixed in some obsessive situation. Even the narrative voices differ. Kees's poetic voice is expan-sive and interpretive; his fictional voice is laconic and clini-cally descriptive. But the stories and the poems do have one crucial similarity. They both reflect the same bleak vision of life. In their carefully-drawn everyday situations and their psychological portraits of "ordinary" individuals, the stories reveal the analytical side of Kees's imagination and show how thoroughly it adapted the mundane reality of his time and place to create a distinctly personal body of work.

Kees's best stories achieve the force and memorability of his finest poems. Now forty years after their initial publication, they still show Kees as a true contemporary. However rooted they are in the particular world of the American 'thirties and 'forties, they present us with a world where nothing is essentially different than today. Even when Kees exploited the ephemera of his era – the intrusion of radio announcements, book titles, newspaper headlines, background music – the results are still remarkably contemporary. His stories do not turn away from the ugliness and brutality of American life, nor do they condone or glorify it. As serious fiction should, his stories take the world in which we live and force us to see it more clearly. While Kees may be faulted for the limited scope of his vision, he is unmatched for the intense accuracy of what he does see. He concentrates on the very subjects we would gladly ignore or turn away from – the ugly, ordinary aspects of modern life – and then reveals how deeply frightening the world we take for granted can be. Above all Kees shows how monstrous and unfeeling it is to be "normal" in American society, and does so with such force that one cannot finish the story without a shock of recognition. This bitter surprise of recognizing the obvious for the first time, of acknowledging our spoiled, egotistic selves, our short, ineffective lives, our fallen world – is the characteristic of all Kees's finest writing, and at their best, his stories deliver it as strongly as his poems. They deserve to be read, and reread. They are an important part of Kees's achievement as a writer, a part of an inheritance which no one has yet assessed or claimed.

IV.

Kees wrote so much fiction that there was a temptation in putting this collection together to include all the short stories to show the range of his interests. Indeed several knowledgeable critics strongly urged me to do so. On consideration, however, it seemed wisest to publish only his best pieces. At this point his reputation would not be served by reprinting work whose only distinction is that it is by Kees. Of the forty-three stories and sketches I have tracked down, about half have enough merit to reprint. Of these I have chosen the fourteen best. Together they give a fairly full representation of Kees's fictional range.

"The Ceremony" and "I Should Worry" show Kees's fiction at its finest. Concise, cruel, and unforgettable, these stories combine psychological insight with a grim sense of social drama. Altogether different is "The Evening of the Fourth of July" which is unique among Kees's stories. Here his savage vision of Depression America has been translated into a bizarre comedy which reveals a sensibility much closer to the poems – a type of fiction that pushes itself forward in brilliant flashes and striking images. Not everyone will appreciate its surreal kind of humor, but readers who find dark comedies like West's *A Cool Million* or Céline's *Journey to the End of the Night* often closer to the truth about modern society than more realistic fiction, will relish Kees's unpatriotic nightmare.

More realistic are "Gents 50¢/Ladies 25¢," "Mrs. Lutz," "So Cold Outside," and "Letter from Maine," which demonstrate Kees's early fascination with regional fiction. These four pieces are laid in Weston, Nebraska, where Kees set about a dozen stories. "Mrs. Lutz" is a cruel portrait of a small-town hypocrite, while "Gents 50¢/Ladies 25¢," with its haunting image of the three haggard women standing like the Fates outside a dancehall, shows an ordinary young woman being smothered by her sordid environment. "So Cold Outside" employs a typically Keesian inversion. The normal people who unfeelingly drive a grotesque and filthy old woman from a heated department store on a cold winter morning are ultimately revealed as the truly contemptible figures of the story. Likewise "Letter from Maine" depicts the archetypal Kees protagonist helplessly trapped in a miserable life.

"Public Library," "The Sign," and "The Library: Four Sketches" each draw in different ways on the six years Kees spent working in the Denver Public Library. Written in 1937 when Kees had just arrived in Denver, the "Four Sketches" are quick satiric portraits of small-town victims and predators. "Public Library," written three years later, is a sophisticated collage of fragmentary observations which combine to depict the institution and its community more complexly than the earlier, more conventional sketches could accomplish in so short a space. Finally, "The Sign" studies the character of a single librarian shown in claustrophobic detail.

The last four stories, "The Brothers," "Do You Like the Mountains?," "Farewell to Frognall," and "The Purcells," show Kees's more relaxed and fluent later style. "The Brothers" depicts another trapped man, this one torn between duty and contempt for his irresponsible younger brother. "Do You Like the Mountains?," Kees's only Hollywood story, is a controlled and understated double portrait of a young would-be actor and an older man obsessed with his dead lover. It hints at the sort of fiction Kees might have gone on to write had he not abandoned the genre. "Farewell to Frognall" is a less accomplished story, an incomplete sketch of a failed intellectual, but despite its shortcomings, it also provides a glimpse into the side of Kees which produced the poems. "The Purcells" was Kees' last story. Seen through the eyes of an uninnocent child, it portrays the grotesque failure of a doomed marriage and, with a few touches from Poe, the fall of a great house. It provides a haunting conclusion to Kees's fictional career. Here then are fourteen stories never collected before and most out of print for forty years. They have waited long enough for readers.

This book would not have been possible without the pioneering work done by Barbara C. Webber. Her preliminary bibliography of Weldon Kees, though incomplete, was the first extensive catalogue of the author's work, and her early unpublished compilation from the stories helped stimulate this selection. The appended checklist of Kees's stories also uses Webber's prior work but rearranges it chronologically, establishes dates for undated publications, and adds one story unknown to her.

I would also like to thank Pamela Gossin along with the other staff members of Heritage Room at the Bennett Martin Library in Lincoln, who oversee the Kees archive, and Raymond Nelson of the University of Virginia who provided me with additional information.

Finally, I would like to thank Harry Duncan who originally commissioned this project six years ago, for Abattoir Editions, his fine press located at the University of Nebraska in Omaha. No author could hope for a more generous publisher or accomplished printer.

DANA GIOIA

SELECTED SHORT STORIES
OF WELDON KEES

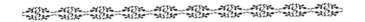

THE CEREMONY

WHEN THE PHONE RANG, Hollenbeck was leaning over his desk looking at a blueprint, his eyes tracing the network of white lines. He let it ring again, and then he looked up, frowning, and resignedly lifted the receiver. Never a moment's peace, he said to himself, never a minute without some sort of interruption. Try to get something done, just try.

"Hello," he said gruffly into the mouthpiece.

"That you, Floyd?" a voice came.

It was Kinnaman. What the hell did he want now? "Yeh," he said.

"Floyd," the voice on the phone whined, "out here a–"

"Yeh," he said helplessly. "What is it? What's the trouble now?"

"You better come out here, Floyd. Murdock and Janss–"

"What about 'em? What's the trouble? Can't you look after that job or do I have to be there every goddamn minute?"

The half-burned cigarette fell off the ashtray. He picked it up from the desk and threw it on the floor and stepped on it.

"Murdock and Janss–"

"Yeh?"

"They won't dig no more. They said–"

"What?" Hollenbeck said. "And just why won't they dig any more?"

"You better come out here. These guys. They said they won't dig no more the way the setup is. You ought to–"

"Well, what's the matter with 'em? For God's sake. They were all right when I left." Hollenbeck paused, staring for a moment at a fly that was buzzing around an apple core on his desk. "Listen, Kinnaman, can't you take care of things? Do I have to look after everything?"

"You better come out here, Floyd," Kinnaman went on. "I can't do nothing with them guys. After they struck the first one—"

"The first one? What're you talking about?"

The phone sounded dead.

"Hey. Hey, Kinnaman."

"Yeh?"

"You there?"

"Yeh, sure. What's the matter?"

"Sounded like the phone was dead."

"No, it's okay. I can hear you fine."

"It just sounded like it was dead for a minute there." He scratched his leg. The fly was still buzzing.

"I'm just telling you, Floyd, I can't argue with these here guys. You better hop in the car and run out here. Janss said—"

"All right, all right," said Hollenbeck. "I'll be out. Keep your shirt on." One thing after another, he thought.

"I just thought," Kinnaman began.

Hollenbeck put down the receiver and lit another cigarette. He just thought, he said to himself. He just thought, did he? Well. He just thought. He stared at the blueprint, thinking: Just when I was beginning to accomplish something. Just when I was getting something done. The fly buzzed near his head and lit on his ear. He swung at it and missed.

Getting up, he put on his hat and coat and went out to the curb where the car was parked. It started easily and he threw it into second and pulled away from the curb. A car with a Florida license plate went by and he looked at it wishing that he was out of the goddamned town and through with it for good. To get away to Florida; fishing. That was the life. Not this. He bore down on the footfeed and turned the corner, heading towards the highway. By the time he struck the gravel, he was doing fifty-five.

He pulled the car into the lot and turned off the ignition and coasted up to the place where they were digging the basement for the barbecue joint. Kinnaman came over to the car and put his foot on the runningboard.

"Well, what's the matter this time?" Hollenbeck said. He saw Janss and Murdock sitting on the ground, their shovels beside them.

"Get out and take a look."

"What's up?"

Kinnaman didn't answer for a minute. Hollenbeck waited impatiently. I haven't got all day, he thought. They think I've got all the time in the world.

"There's bodies here," Kinnaman said finally.

"What?"

"Bodies. Indian bodies. Petrified."

"What the hell are you talking about, Kinnaman?"

"It's a fact. They're petrified. There used to be an Indian cemetery or something around here. We struck one of them while we was digging and now Janss and Murdock don't want to dig no more."

"What the hell's the matter with 'em. Why won't they dig?"

"They're scared," Kinnaman said. "Don't ask me. Hell, it ain't no fault of mine, Floyd."

"What are they scared of?" Hollenbeck said. Damned ignorant fools, he thought. Those things wouldn't hurt them. Vaguely he remembered that someone had told him once of an Indian burial ground someplace in the vicinity.

"Those guys," Kinnaman said. "They say you shouldn't go

5

fooling around with dead bodies, even if they're petrified. I can't do nothing with 'em."

"Jesus Christ," Hollenbeck said. But he didn't feel like getting out of the car. "Listen, Kinnaman, can't you take care of things? Can't I leave for a couple of minutes without something going haywire out here? Or do I have to stand over you guys every minute?"

Kinnaman shrugged his shoulders. "You better talk to 'em. Maybe you can do something with 'em."

"I'll do something with them, all right." He got out of the car and slammed the door. Kicking at the sandy soil, he walked beside Kinnaman to where the two men were sitting. He stared at the flat landscape, wondering what new grief he would have to put up with tomorrow. There was always something.

When they came up, Janss and Murdock stood and nodded to Hollenbeck.

"Well, what's the matter with you guys?" Hollenbeck said.

Janss looked up at him as if he didn't want to say anything. He was a short man with a scar on his forehead. "It's them bodies. We don't want to fool with them."

"Yeh," Murdock said. "That monkeying around with dead people. You can't ask a guy to do that, Mr. Hollenbeck."

What am I paying you guys for, that's what I want to know, Hollenbeck thought. Not to sit around and beef. "Where is this body, anyway?" he asked.

"Over there."

They went over to where they had been digging. Murdock pointed at something that looked to Hollenbeck like a slab of stone.

He got down on his haunches and looked at it closely. It was a petrified man, all right. The first he'd ever seen, except for one in a museum, years ago in Chicago. He felt of the thing, and it gave him a queer sensation when his hands touched it. Like death. He looked up, trying to shake off the feeling he had, trying to appear as tough as he could, and said, "Well, what of it? Break it up and get it out of here. What am I paying you guys for?"

The men didn't answer him. He stood up and looked angrily at their faces, thinking: Say something, one of you guys, say something.

"Break it up and get it out of here, I said. You guys want these jobs, don't you? Or maybe I got you all wrong. Maybe you'd like to find something else that'd be more genteel or something. Come on, get going."

Janss cleared his throat and looked at Murdock. There was a long silence, and then both of them began to speak at once. They looked at each other confusedly and stopped.

"Well, how about it? If you lay down on this, I'll promise you that you'll never get any work from me or anybody else in this town. Get that? Know what I mean?"

"But dead people," Janss said. Murdock stared at the ground.

"So damn dead they've turned to stone," Hollenbeck said. "Come on, break the thing up and get it out of here."

No answer.

"I got better things to do than run out here every ten minutes to straighten out things like this. Well, you going to get back to work, or not?"

Janss and Murdock exchanged glances.

"Okay," Murdock said. "All right with you, Janss?"

"Yeh."

"I hate to beg you," Hollenbeck said sarcastically. "There's plenty of guys who wouldn't put up with such a goddamn fuss about some piece of rock. But we got a barbecue stand to put up here. Maybe you forgot about that?"

"Okay, okay," Murdock said. "Where's them sledge-hammers?"

Hollenbeck watched the men as they went over to the truck to get them. "Crazy bastards," he said to Kinnaman.

"Yeh."

"Scared of a piece of rock. Imagine."

"Yeh."

"It's really kind of funny."

"Yeh, it is, kind of."

The men returned, lugging the heavy hammers. They carried them over to the petrified Indian.

"Now break it up good," said Hollenbeck. They were nuts the fuss they made. Wasting all this time of his.

"Yeh, break it up good," Kinnaman repeated.

The men raised their hammers and swung them down. At the first blow, the body cracked. Hollenbeck stood there, shading his eyes from the sun with his hand. One less petrified Indian. The next time the hammers descended there were four large pieces and other little ones, crumbling.

"The vanishing American," Hollenbeck said.

"Huh?" said Kinnaman.

Hollenbeck laughed. That was good, really good. It hadn't sounded so funny until he said it. And it had come out, just like that, all of a sudden.

"The vanishing American," Hollenbeck said again. "Get it?"

Kinnaman laughed too. "Say, that's good!" he said. "That's all right. That's really all right, boss."

Hollenbeck couldn't get over how funny it was. He laughed harder. The vanishing American. And it had come to him, just like that. Without thinking about it at all.

"Jesus, that's really good, Floyd!" Kinnaman said.

The blows of the hammers kept coming down, even, regular, on the crumbling pieces of stone. Dust rose in the air in a little cloud, drifting slowly down.

"That's really good, Floyd," said Kinnaman, his sides shaking.

"That's about the funniest thing I've heard in a long time."

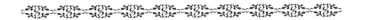

I SHOULD WORRY

ARCH BOYLE lounged in a broken wicker chair in front of his used auto parts place. A half-smoked cigarette was pasted in one corner of his mouth, and from the other corner a broken toothpick hung. Across the street, in front of the City Mission, an old man was sweeping the sidewalk with a worn broom. A bunch of kids were rollerskating, and each time they went by, the old man had to stop sweeping, leaning on his broom until they had passed. The wheels of their skates rasped on the concerete and, whenever they rolled over divisions in the sidewalk, they made a clacking sound like a needle on a cracked Victrola record. The old man would watch them and then return to his work, raising a thin sift of dust.

Arch deftly removed the toothpick without putting his hands to his face or disturbing the cigarette, and again he thought of his sister. Now, he thought, she would be standing in front of the mirror in the room above him, the room in which his parents had killed themselves, and she would be combing her hair with one hand, her eyes wandering from her distorted image to the pictures of movie actors that she had torn from magazines and pasted on the wall. He could see her vividly, even the sling around her neck, and he wondered if she would be coming down before long.

He changed his position in the chair, trying to keep his eyes out of the sunlight without going back into the store

9

too far. It was an open-front place: all kinds of used auto parts were scattered over shelves and boxes and tables. He got into a comfortable position, and after he was settled, he crossed his legs and began to strike himself below the knee-cap with the side of his hand. He was testing his reflexes.

Satisfied that they were all right, same as they'd been yesterday, he began thinking of how much he wanted a drink of gin. He wanted a drink in the worst way, but that morning he had paid O. B. Daniels the rent on the building, and now he was flat. He didn't have a cent, and there hadn't been any business all day. It was getting close to five o'clock, and he was broke and needed a shot of gin. Better yet, two shots. He wished he had held out a little on O. B.

Next door at Womack's American Radio Repair Shop, a loudspeaker blared the final chorus of *The Love Bug Will Bite You If You Don't Watch Out*. Arch tapped his foot in time to the music, imagining a scene in which he talked O. B. into lowering the rent. *You are listening to "The World Dances," a group of recorded numbers by Howard Griffin and his Californians. We hear them next in an interrogative mood, as they ask the musical question, "Am I Wasting My Time?"* Or better yet: say he had something on O. B. Listen, O. B., I know all about this little graft you're working and maybe some other people'd like to know about it too. Huh? O. B. looked green around the gills. Well, what is it you want, Boyle? The rent on the building. That's all. O. B. not liking it but agreeing. He had to. Shaking his head, saying okay. A cinch.

Nuts.

He took a last drag from his cigarette and tossed it on the sidewalk. It rolled along, scattering sparks, then fell off the curb into the gutter. He yawned, wondering why Womack had to play that thing so loud all the time. Made so much noise you couldn't hear yourself think.

People went by: an old man in his shirtsleeves carrying a basket, a fat Negress in a violet dress who dragged along with one hand a little colored kid, a boy on a red bicycle, two young fellows in overalls carrying dinnerpails. As they passed, one of them said, They ain't going to get me over there, hell no. Two dogs trotted by, their noses to the ground. They paused for a moment in front of Arch to sniff at a red popbottle cap on the sidewalk, and then went on, their tails held stiff and erect.

Arch got up and stretched. His shirtsleeves were rolled up above his elbows, and the wicker chair had left a mottled red print on his fat arms, corrugating them like a washboard. He walked over to Womack's American Radio Repair Shop and looked inside.

Womack! he yelled.

The radio was playing so loudly that his voice could scarcely be heard. The funnel-shaped loudspeaker boomed from above the doorway. Tendrils of wires escaped from its base through little holes bored in the wood.

Womack! he called again.

Finally a man came up from the cellar. He was carrying a pair of pliers. He looked up, frowning slightly, and said, What'd ya want? He stood there, the trapdoor behind him, looking first at Arch and then at the pliers in his hand.

Turn that thing down, can you? Arch said. I bet you can hear it clear over in the next block.

What's the matter? Don't you like it?

What'd you think?

That's what I'm asking you. He put the pliers down on a workbench.

Jesus, you can hear it for blocks. Why don't you turn it down?

Because maybe I want it loud, that's why.

Holy God, Arch thought. What can you do with a guy like him?

Womack came over close to him and tapped him on the chest with a pudgy forefinger. Listen, he said slowly, I play it loud on account of a good reason, see? Music's something people like to hear. I give 'em music. Music plays. Gives me more business, get the point?

Okay, okay. Only turn it down. You don't know what a racket that thing makes. A guy has to sit out there and listen to it. You can hear it for blocks.

And maybe I like it that way.

You must, Arch said. Listen, Womack, look at it this way. It stands to reason that nobody wants their eardrums ruined. That ain't going to get you no business. Sure, give 'em music, but turn it down. Jesus, I bet you can hear it clear over on Christopher Street.

Womack scratched his head.

Hell, it just stands to reason nobody wants their eardrums ruined. That's just sense.

Maybe so, Womack said.

It's just sense, that's all.

Okay, I'll turn it down a little. I guess it won't hurt none.

A guy just can't hear himself think the way it's going now, Arch said. Say, Womack . . .

Yeh?

You couldn't loan a guy a dollar, could you. Until Monday?

No, I couldn't, said Womack.

I didn't think you could, Arch said. Okay. Forget it.

I wasn't even thinking about it none.

Okay. Okay. I just thought.

Well, think again, said Womack.

He left him regulating the volume on the radio. Arch's sister, Betty Lou, had come down from their rooms over the shop, and now she sat in the wicker chair, a green knit dress stretched tight over her body. She had broken her arm about a week before. It hung in a white sling that was tied around her neck.

Arch looked at her, wishing he were over at Freddie's picking up a couple of straight gins. He didn't say anything.

She stared up at him, her jaws working at a piece of gum she had just started on. He was close enough to her to get a whiff of the wintergreen odor. She was deaf and dumb.

He wondered again just how she had broken her arm. All he knew was that some guy in a green sedan had picked her up last Thursday late in the evening, and when she had come back, alone, three or four hours later, she had a broken arm. She was whimpering, and she held her arm out to him, shaking her head and sobbing soundlessly. He had set it himself – doctors were too expensive – working carefully with the splints to make sure it would be all right.

Later, he had tried to get it out of her, tried to find out how it had happened. Time after time he had poked the piece of paper in front of her, the piece of paper on which he had written: *How did it happen? You better tell me.* He had put the pencil between her fingers, commanding her to write, but she had repeatedly thrown it on the floor, shaking her head and stamping her feet. He hadn't been able to get a thing out of her since it had happened. And now she sat there in the wicker chair, her jaws moving regularly behind the slash of scarlet on her lips that broke the paleness of her face, her green dress pulled up just a little too high, watching the cars that were going by in the five o'clock rush.

If my mother and the old man had lived, he thought. All right: break your goddamn arm, go ahead. See if I care. He put a cigarette between his lips and struck a match on his beltbuckle. Break your arm, he thought.

Womack hadn't turned down the radio so that you could notice it . . . *presenting a group of recorded selections by Howard Griffin and his Californians. Here's an old favorite for you! It's Howard Griffin's interpretation of "Ida." A recording.*

Maybe some people have lives that make sense, he thought. Maybe some of them do things that make some difference, maybe for some of them it goes some place and has some meaning. More meaning than getting up in the hot or the cold morning, it doesn't make any difference, and putting on a pair of dirty socks and clothes that you wore yesterday and eating breakfast with a sister that can't hear you or speak to you. And all of the time you're wondering what's going on in her mind. And then you go to the shop and wait on customers, if you're lucky enough to have any, and then by the time night comes around you toss a slug of gin inside of you and after you're good and drunk you fall into bed dog-tired and feel it spinning around beneath you and hear the streetcars rumbling by in the dark and your head feeling like a bomb about to explode.

He went towards the back of the shop and dug around in some rubbish to see if he could find a bottle that he might have overlooked. They were all empties, though. He stood for a moment by the dirty window. Some kids walked up the alley, kicking a tin can. You going to the movies tonight? Nah. And the can banging on the concrete. He tapped the ash from the cigarette. If I only had some dough, he thought. If I only had a little dough.

An automobile pulled up in front of the place, and without turning he knew by the sound of the motor that it was a Chevy, probably a 1934 model. When he heard the door of the car click shut, he looked around and saw a man in a gray suit walking towards him.

You got any straps for license plates? the man asked.

Arch looked him over. He was wearing a gray felt hat and a gray suit and limped slightly. He was about forty or so, Arch guessed.

Yeh. Right over here.

Arch led him to a table and indicated the straps. But the man wasn't looking at the merchandise on the table; instead, he was standing in the aisle watching Betty Lou. She was looking at him, too, her eyes half closed and one leg crossed over the other, swinging it slowly up and down.

Here they are, Arch said.

Huh? the man said, glancing up. Oh yeh, the straps. He glanced back at the girl for a moment and then fastened his eyes on the straps. How much? I only need one. The one on the front plate just broke.

Well, here's one I'll sell you for a dime. It's used a little.

The man looked at it briefly, holding it in his hands, and said, That's all right. I'll take it. I'll take this one. He fished a dime from his pocket, and dropped it in Arch's hand. There you are, he said. Then his eyes went back to Betty Lou. His tongue kept going over his lower lip, slowly moistening it.

I've done it before, Arch thought. But never when she's had a broken arm. But I could use the dough, and she doesn't care. It's nothing to her. A thing like that.

Something else? Arch said.

The man started. No, huhuh, I guess not.

Interested in the girl?

The man laughed nervously.

Betty Lou was half turned in the wicker chair, staring at the man, smiling. Her crossed leg moved up and down regularly.

Two bucks, mister, said Arch.

The man raised an eyebrow. Two? he said. What's the matter with her arm?

It's sprained. Don't worry about that. It won't bother you none. You ain't worrying about that, are you?

The man slapped the strap softly against his leg. *For the past thirty minutes you have been listening to a group of dance selections played by Howard Griffin and his Californians.* The man looked at Arch and then at the girl.

The wicker chair squeaked faintly as she rocked back and forth. The green dress was tight as a bathing suit.

You can go upstairs if you want to, Arch said. How about it?

Well...

Two bucks, said Arch. You can give the money to me. Arch stepped on the cigarette, two faint spirals of smoke escaping from his nostrils. Come on, he thought. For God's sake. Make up your mind. I'm not going to beg you.

The man smiled slightly. Make it a dollar and a half.

Two. Now, honest, ain't it worth that?

Dollar and a half. What the hell. A sprained arm...

Okay, Arch said slowly. Make it a dollar seventy-five. That's fair enough. He stuck his hand in his pockets, feeling the large hole in the bottom of the one on the left side.

The man glanced quickly at the girl and said, All right. Dollar seventy-five. You get the money, you say?

That's right.

Arch took the crumpled dollar bill, holding it in his palm while the man placed the coins over the smooth engraved face of George Washington. Arch nodded to Betty Lou. He watched her get up and come to the man and smile at him, the red smear crawling up both sides of her cheeks, taking his arm and looking up into his face.

She's a dummy, Arch said.

What? the man said. I don't get it. The smile he had arranged on his face for the girl began to fade.

She's deaf and dumb, Arch said. That's all. Not that it makes any difference to you, I suppose.

The man shook his head. Deaf and dumb?

That's right, Arch said.

And then Betty Lou was pulling the man towards the door that led to the rooms above. He could hear their footsteps on the stairs. It was beginning to get dark. People were coming home from work and the streetcars went by, one after another.

He went to the front of the store and began to pull the large folding doors together, getting ready to close up for the night. One dime taken in, he thought. One dime and a dollar seventy-five. I'll put the dollar in my shoe for groceries so we'll have enough to eat on, until something turns up, and I'll get drunk on the eighty-five. I'll get drunk and come home from Freddie's with my head going around and around and then it won't make any difference. Nothing. It doesn't make any difference anyway. It made some difference a long time ago, maybe seven or eight years ago, but that was when I had a lot of different ideas than I have now. Goofy ideas. When I thought that maybe there was something to it.

I should worry about her. He took the padlock and snapped it shut over the opening between the two doors. I should worry about her, broken arm and all . . . *the weather forecast for tonight is fair and warmer in the southern part of the state. For Tuesday . . .*

The closed doors shut out all light except for the faint blue blur that hung in a square in back: the barred window. He felt his way through the store's darkness and opened the rear door. Before he closed it, he felt in his pocket to make sure that he had the keys with him.

I should worry about her. Because that's all she knows. Because it's been that way since the two of them stuffed the door of the living room with newspapers and turned on the gas and waited there, sitting in the chairs by the window, with that slow hissing sound all around them. And the smell getting stronger all the time. Because that's the way it's been ever since then with her. I tried to stop her too many times and then I gave up.

He felt for cigarettes, but there weren't any left. I'll get some when I get to Freddie's. In the alley, the telephone wires hummed above him. Some kid had drawn something on the side of one of the buildings, but he couldn't make out what it was. I gave it up a long time ago. He turned where the alley met the street and walked without haste to the corner, waiting for a moment for the lights to change from red to green before he crossed to the other side.

GENTS 50¢ / LADIES 25¢

DORAJEAN MELTZER was sitting on a high stool in the Roseland Gardens ticket booth. She had her neck turned back as far as she could and through the isinglass window in the door she could get a good view of the whole dance floor with the couples swinging around to the last chorus of *All My Life*. From behind the faded pink crepepaper fringe that bordered the orchestra's platform, the bassplayer smiled broadly and swung his arm out and back and out and back. The bassplayer was a cute boy, Dorajean mused; he was cute all right. He had a cute smile. She swung one of her shapely legs back and forth in time with the rhythm. Dorajean thought, gee, it was no fun being cooped up in an old ticket booth when everybody else was having fun.

"How about it, baby, do I get ticket or don't I get ticket?"

She jerked her head around quickly and saw a drunk waving a soiled dollar bill towards her. He was a fat old thing, she thought; it was perfectly disgusting the way these fat old men would come out to the Roseland and try to get fresh with young girls. She ripped a ticket from the roll that hung from a nail by the window and shoved it towards him. She put the bill in the drawer and gave him fifty cents.

"Time's it?" the fat man said. "Time's it getting to be?"

It wasn't any of her business whether he knew the time or not. She was hired to sell tickets and that was all.

"I don't have the time," she said coldly, remembering how

Ann Harding had replied to a man who had bothered her in that picture she had seen at the Isis the night before.

The fat man rubbed his hands over his eyes and looked at her. He swayed slightly and took hold of the wooden railing back of him. It creaked a little.

"Got just much right to be here's anybody else," he said. "Parked car down front of drugstore. Got a perfect right. Much's anybody else."

He had better get inside and quit annoying her, Dorajean thought. These greasy fat men that came out to the park and fooled around inside the dancehall were the worst ever. She watched him blink his eyes as he stared at the orange ticket.

"River-view Park," he read slowly. "Roseland Gardens. Admit one." He wrinkled his forehead and looked at her curiously, as if seeing her for the first time. "I got just good right to be here's anybody else," he said, starting for the dance floor. "I don't have to take that stuff off nobody. Parked m'car." She watched him go inside and stand uncertainly, blinking his eyes.

Dorajean held her head as high as she could, looking out across the dark stretch of ground between the dancehall and the swimming pool to the long row of automobiles that lined the driveway. She was Ann Harding now, glorious blond Ann, and she didn't have crooked teeth or a nose that was too pointed. She was Ann Harding, and Ronald Colman was just about to ask her to go away with him in his Packard convertible. "I belong to you alone, Ronald," Dorajean Meltzer whispered to herself. "We are one forever and a day."

Behind her, Ted Pope and his Serenaders broke into *Who's Sorry Now?* with the trombone carrying the melody. Dorajean stopped being Ann Harding and began to think about the bassplayer in Ted Pope's band. He was cute. She craned her neck around again to look at the orchestra. They looked keen in their gray double-breasted suits and their burgundy-colored shirts and yellow neckties. It was a swell band, the best the park had booked since Morry Edwards and his Swinging Serenaders had been there. That had been about a month ago, on Art's night off.

Dorajean swung her leg in time to the music. She tried to sing the words, but she couldn't remember them. Something about whose heart is aching for breaking each vow. Something like that.

The bassplayer was a lot cuter than Art Daub, the fellow she went out with. Art was all right, but wasn't handsome or polished and he didn't say romantic things or have a keen personality like the bassplayer. She felt lonely sitting in the booth all by herself, and just the same she would be glad to see Art when he got off work at the flour mill at eleven. He would have flour in his ears and in the little wrinkles around his eyes. Art smelled of flour.

She wished that the bassplayer would ask her for a date, because she thought he was cute. Dorajean just knew that she could fall for a boy like him; she could fall hard for a boy like that, a boy who had a slick personality and curly brown hair. But her brother Mort had told her he would take a strap to her if he so much as caught her talking to a musician. Mort had played with Jimmy Unthank and his Orchestra for a while, and Mort said musicians were all a bunch of chasers and only out after one thing and that was all they thought of. Mort had his good times, though, Dorajean noticed. He just didn't want her to have a good time, she thought. He was mean, that was all; he was just plain mean.

From around the corner of the buidling she saw three women appear, their shadows long and slender on the gravel. The women were all young, but thin and undernourished. They wore cheap print dresses and one of them was carrying a baby.

They lived down the road about half a mile from the park,

and every now and then they would come down to the Roseland and stand outside and watch the dancers. Dorajean
Meltzer knew who they were: the wives of some men who
worked on the night shift at the factory out by the U.P.
tracks. Dorajean wished that they wouldn't come to the
dancehall and stand outside and look in at the dancers the
way they did; it gave her a funny uncomfortable feeling she
couldn't understand. She wished that they would go away.
She didn't like them being around.

A few feet from the pavilion there was a little mound of
earth where it had not been smoothed level, and from there
you could look into the dancehall. You could see inside
pretty well from there. Dorajean watched the three women
standing out there on the little mound, the shortest one on
tiptoe holding her baby. The baby began to cry and the
woman frowned and said something to it.

Ted Pope and his Serenaders swung into *Stompin' at the
Savoy*. They could really play, all right. Dorajean Meltzer
wished for the fiftieth time that evening that she was out on
the floor dancing with some real keen dancer like Harold
Latenz. Only Art didn't like to have her dance with Harold
Latenz; he said he didn't like the way he danced. Dorajean
knew what he meant, but she didn't say anything. She
couldn't have any fun at all. She felt very sorry for herself.
Gee, *Stompin' at the Savoy* was such a keen tune to dance to,
and she had to sit in the ticket booth, even though the dance
was over half finished and nobody was buying tickets
anymore.

Looking at the three women, Dorajean began to think that
they were only a few years older than she was, five or six or
seven years perhaps, and already they were thin and
unattractive and cross-looking. They had just let themselves
go. But that wasn't true; her mother was still a young
woman, really, and for years she had looked like they did.

They all got to look that way. Dorajean thought there was something about being poor and having to struggle for a living that took their youth and their good looks away from them in no time. In just no time at all. It would happen to her, too, she thought sadly.

Dorajean refused to think about it any longer. It was just morbid to think about it. She wouldn't think about it. I won't get to look that way, she told herself; I won't, I won't; I'll marry a young man with lots and lots of money and I'll have all kinds of beauty treatments and I'll be young and pretty, even if my teeth are a little crooked. She would have them straightened. She thought of herself sitting in a chair, something like a dentist's chair, only different and a lot more elaborate than that, and the nice doctor who looked a little like Ronald Colman only more like Clark Gable, would be saying: "There you are, Miss Meltzer." And he handed her a mirror, and there were her teeth, just as even and pearly as that girl's in the Pepsodent ads.

Only it wasn't so. Behind her they were playing the middle part of *Stompin' at the Savoy* with a heavy downbeat, the brasses blasting the lead. One of the three women out on the mound was beating time with her foot. Dorajean could see their lips moving, they were saying something; but with the band making so much noise, it was like watching a silent movie.

A fellow and a girl came out of the dancehall, and the fellow said loud enough for Dorajean to hear him: "Listen here, Marge, if you think you can pull any of that stuff on me and get away with it, you're just crazier than hell!" They stood there on the narrow platform outside, glaring at each other. "Oh, shut up," the girl said. "You shut up." The man took her by the arm and pulled her down the stairs. The girl struck at him. "Let go of me, goddammit," the girl cried out. Then he pulled her harder, and said something else, but

Dorajean couldn't make out what it was he was saying. She saw them walk toward the row of automobiles, the man dragging the girl, their shadows stretching endlessly in front of them.

Dorajean made a noise with her tongue: *tk, tk.* She opened the door to the booth and called to Les Baker, the fellow who took tickets.

"What time is it, Les?"

"Wouldn't you like to know?" Les said, taking his Ingersoll out of his vest pocket. "Wouldn't you like to know, though?" He grinned at her. "Always wanting to know what time it is, aren't you?"

Les was always kidding, Dorajean thought. He was a great one for kidding.

"Come on, Les," she pleaded. "What time is it, really?"

He peered at the cracked watchface for a long time, wrinkling his forehead.

"Yes, sir," he said, putting the watch back in his pocket. "I should say so."

"Aw, Les," Dorajean said. "Tell me what time it is. I want to know. Please."

"I just can't turn you down, I guess," Les said. "It's a quarter past eleven. To the minute."

"Thanks." She opened the drawer and scooped up the coins and bills and put them in a sack and gave them to Les.

"Pretty good take," he said.

"Not bad."

"Yeh, a pretty good take," he said.

"It's not so bad," she said.

She closed the door and looked out to the drive to see if Art's car was in sight yet. She couldn't see him and she wondered what was holding him up.

Those three women were still there. Dorajean wished they would go away and stay away. She imagined herself as one of them, married (*Mrs. Arthur Daub*), her husband working nights, coming out to the Roseland with some other women, standing out there on that old mound. She couldn't stand thinking about it. It wasn't going to be that way: it wasn't! Only it would be that way if she married Art, and if she didn't what else could she do but just go on selling tickets, night after night after night.

What got her started thinking that way? She wished Art would hurry up and come so that they could get out of the park and ride in the cool night air. It was a keen night. It would be swell to ride and feel the wind going through her hair.

One of the boys in the band was singing a chorus, but she wasn't listening to him. She wished she could feel good again. Most of the time she felt swell, but now she felt just terrible. She wished she could be somebody else instead of being Dorajean Meltzer. It wasn't any fun being herself. She had never felt this way before; it was a different feeling that was strange and awful. She didn't know what it was at all.

I can't go on with just mem-o-reeees, the boy sang.

Dorajean turned around to see who was singing. It was the cute bassplayer, but she couldn't get so excited about him now. She wondered why that was. She couldn't figure it out. All of a sudden she was aware that she was tired, terribly tired. Her ears hummed. All up and down her spine there was an ache.

Although I know I'll never forget you, the boy sang.

She turned around to see if Art had driven up in his car yet. There were headlights shining on the drive, but they weren't his. His were sort of yellowish, and these were white and blinding. Then she saw his lights preceding the car through the gray gate with the sign: *Weston Riverview Park. Fun for the Whole Family.* The lights came closer slowly. Art was a careful driver, Dorajean thought: that was one thing about him.

The women were not there any longer. For a long time she stared at the place they had been. They must have left the last time when I turned around, she thought. They must have left then.

She couldn't get them out of her mind. She kept seeing herself in a dirty cotton housedress with her skin stretched tightly over the bones of her face, with her mouth drawn and hard.

She took out her doreen and looked at her face for a long time in the small powder-dusted mirror. "I won't get to look that way," she said; "I won't get to look that way." She daubed some powder on her nose and blinked at herself in the mirror. "I won't," she said to herself, "I won't."

Art's car moved into a vacant stall. Dorajean thought that it was funny how you thought things about cars at night. When you saw them moving, then you never thought of them as being driven by people. They seemed to move all by themselves. It was funny, all right.

She wanted to cry, and she felt more tired than ever. Seeing Art getting out of the car and coming towards her she wanted to shout at him and tell him to go away. Only she wanted to cry on his shoulder. She couldn't understand why she felt the way she did; she had never felt that way before in all her life.

Art's shoes kicked up little gray clouds of dust as he walked towards the pavilion. He looked tired, too, Dorajean thought. He looks awful tired.

He came up onto the platform.

"How's the kid?" he said, smiling at her.

She slipped off the high stool and put on her hat.

"I want you to go fast," she said crazily. "I want to go fast in the car."

"That's what it's for," he said.

"I want to go Fast, Art," she said. "Fast."

"Anything you say, Dorajean," Art said.

"I feel funny, Art. I feel sort of funny. I don't know why it is. I don't feel so good."

"You look kind of tired," he said.

"I don't know what's the matter with me."

She wanted to cry and she wanted to laugh and she wanted to scream something at Art, scream at him; but instead she opened the door of the booth quietly and came around and took hold of his arm and smiled at him. She felt like crying, sort of. The orchestra was playing *China Boy.* Walking down the steps, she heard him say: "A darn funny thing happened down at the mill tonight...."

His words went on and on and on; she wasn't even listening to him.

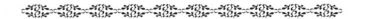

SO COLD OUTSIDE

IT WAS CERTAINLY a bad day at the store, just no business at all. Down in the men's lavatory, George W. Spencer, manager of the shoe department, read in the morning *Journal-Times* that the mercury had reached the lowest point since the February of the winter before. George wished he had had the sense to have his house weatherstripped when his wife had been at him every minute to have it done. It sure looked as though their coal bill was going to be a big one this winter. If it wasn't money for one thing, it was another, he thought. Wish I could get out of this country and go to Florida or California or some place like that.

In the paper it told about a blizzard that was on its way from the northwest. George shivered. The cement floor was like ice. He noticed a story about impassable roads all over the state, and another concerning the difficulty trains were having in getting through. Enough of that depressing stuff, he figured. He turned to the back page and started on the comics. He read Little Orphan Annie, Mutt and Jeff, The Gumps, Moon Mullins, and Tarzan. He guessed he couldn't take the time to read the sports just then; he'd have to save that until lunch.

While he was washing his hands with the liquid soap that smelled like licorice, the janitor came in carrying a mop.

"Hello, George," he said.

"Hello, Ed."

"Cold enough for you?"

"It's cold enough for me," George said, rinsing his hands under the cold water faucet.

"Pretty hard heating this place this kind of weather," the janitor said.

"I bet," George said. He dried his hands on a paper towel. WHY USE TWO WHEN ONE WILL DO? the little brass plate on the container read. George used four, wadding up the damp sheets and throwing them at the wire basket under the washbowl. Only one of them went in; the others rolled jerkily on the floor and stopped.

"Yeh," Ed said, "it's pretty hard heating up a store this size in this kind of weather."

"I bet," George said without interest. He stood close to the water-specked mirror and glared at himself sternly, turning his head from one side to another. Then he took a comb from his pocket and slicked his hair down expertly with some water. Even the water seemed colder than usual. "Yeh, it must be," he said, going out of the washroom.

He went along through the furnace room, humming a little, into the bargain basement where the signs announced in red and black letters a midwinter sale of splendid values in overshoes of unsurpassed quality. George nodded to Merton Burwell and went up the creaking stairs to the first floor.

He stopped at the glove counter to josh Lela Mucheson. Lela was a great kid. George noticed that she was wearing that good-looking green wool outfit that had been in the window before Christmas. He remembered that it had been marked down from $18.50 to $11.95. Lela looked darn good in green.

"Well, aren't we looking spiffy this morning," George said affably, leaning on the counter. He took a stick of gum from his pocket.

"Are we?" Lela cracked back brightly.

George unwrapped the gum and put it in his mouth and began to chew vigorously. "Well, maybe I wouldn't be the one to say," he said.

"Why not?"

"Well, maybe I just wouldn't be the one to say," George said.

"Aren't you going to give me a stick of gum, George?" Lela said. "You don't need to be so stingy."

"My last stick, Lela," George said.

"Well, am *I* disappointed!" Lela said. "To think you'd let me down like that."

George smiled, thinking that Lela was certainly a great kid. Sure a shame that he was married and that she went with that college guy.

"Say, George, I've got a good story to tell you," Lela said.

"Yeah? Well, let's have it, kiddo. You know there's nothing I like better than a good story."

"Not right now." She looked up and suddenly nudged George. "There's that awful woman again," she said. "See her?"

George glanced around but he couldn't see anybody. He didn't know whom Lela was talking about. "What woman?" he said. "Where? I don't see any woman."

"Look," Lela said. "There."

"I don't see any woman."

"Where I'm pointing," Lela said.

George finally made her out. It was hard for him to see any distance without his glasses, and he took them out of his pocket and put them on. He stared at a dowdy-looking woman in a worn cloth coat. She was standing by one of the counters down the aisle a little way fingering a gray sweater-coat. Her hands were very thin and the blue veins in them were corded thickly like a bunch of tangled wires. The seams in her cheap cotton stockings twisted up her skinny legs below a frayed blue skirt.

"Three times I've asked her if she wanted anything and she wouldn't even take the hint," Lela went on. "She's been in here for the last two hours. Two hours! Imagine!"

"The last two hours!" George exclaimed. "What doing?" He watched the woman as she walked away from the sweater counter and stood hesitantly in the aisle as if she didn't know what to do.

"That's what I'd like to know," Lela said. "A person's sure got a lot of nerve to hang around the store like that."

"Two hours!" George said. He couldn't get over it. "That's almost as long as the store's been open this morning."

"I saw her just a little while after the store opened, George," Lela said. "And I said to Kitty when I first saw her, 'Kitty, did you ever see such a sight in your whole life?' And we kept watching her – you know, at first we got sort of a kick out of her, she's so funny-looking and all."

"Maybe she's a shoplifter," George said.

"That's just what I've been thinking."

"They better keep an eye on her."

"Well, I'll just bet you're right about that, George," Lela said. "It wouldn't surprise me if she was a shoplifter."

George looked back to the shoe department, but there wasn't anything doing there. "How about that story you were going to tell me?" he said.

Lela opened her mouth to say something, but just then a customer came up and Lela nodded for George to leave. He walked back to the shoe department, feeling thwarted because Lela hadn't had a chance to tell her story. He hadn't heard a real good story in a long time.

II

After Lela had finished waiting on her customer and sent up her sale's slip, she walked across the aisle to the next counter to talk to Grace Wright. The customer had irritated Lela: she hadn't known what size gloves she had wanted, and she had kept saying over and over, "I just wish I knew which size my sister wears; I never can remember." Lela said to herself that the woman would probably be back with them in a few days, wanting to exchange them for a different size.

Grace was sorting out some stockings. Lela noticed that Grace certainly needed something done to her hair. Well, ever since Grace had got married, she had sort of let herself go; she wasn't anywhere near as neat about herself as she had been before she married Howard Wright. Someone ought to say something to her.

"Gosh," Grace said to her as she came up, "did you ever see it so quiet in the store as it is this morning?"

"It's so cold out," Lela said. "I just about froze to death coming down to work this morning."

"Howard couldn't even get the car started," Grace said. "He tried and tried and tried but he couldn't seem to get it started, and so we had to leave it there in the garage. We almost missed the streetcar."

"I thought I'd just about freeze coming down to work," Lela said. "When I got downtown it was so cold I was just about ready to scream."

Grace arranged one of the piles of stockings. "I can't understand why Howard doesn't get our car fixed," she said. "Every time we really need it this cold weather, he can't get it to start."

"Well, honestly," Lela said, "you can't blame people for not coming downtown on a day like this."

Grace began to put the stockings into boxes and put them back on the shelves. Lela said to herself that Grace certainly needed something done to her hair; it looked perfectly frightful.

"We had to run for the streetcar," Grace said. "For a while I didn't know whether we were going to catch it or not, and I was just sure we weren't going to."

Lela reached down the neck of her dress to pull up one of her shoulder straps. "Grace," she said.

"Huh?"

"Grace, have you noticed that dreadful old woman that's been walking around the store?"

"Noticed her? How could I help it? If she's been by here once she's been by here fifty times."

"I'll just bet you anything she's a shoplifter," Lela said.

"I wouldn't be the least bit surprised," Grace said. "She certainly looks it. Somebody ought to say something to Mr. Thompson. They really ought to."

"You just feel as if you have to keep your eye on her every minute," Lela said. She watched a chilled-looking man in a heavy overcoat come in and go over to the men's department. He was wearing a derby hat. Looked a little like her Uncle Phil, Lela thought. Only Uncle Phil was more heavy-set. "I've only had three sales this morning," she said.

"Three!" Grace said. "Well, you're lucky. I've only had two."

"Only two? Honestly, is that all you've had?"

"I've only had two. Gosh, isn't that awful?" Grace pushed back a strand of hair that had fallen over her forehead.

Lela looked around the store. She wondered if Dale would call her up tonight. She didn't want to just hang around home. She wished there was a good dance to go to. They hadn't been to a dance for almost two weeks. Lela caught a glimpse of the old woman again.

"There she is," Lela said.

"Where?"

"Coming up the stairs from the basement. See her?"

"She's just all over the store, isn't she?" Grace said. They both thought that was pretty funny and they laughed about it for awhile.

"Maybe she thinks this is a museum or something," Lela said. "Honestly, Grace, I just have half a mind to tell Mr. Thompson."

"Well why don't you?" Grace said. "Why don't you?"

"I've half a mind to."

"I would."

"I've certainly got a good notion to," Lela said.

Lela watched the woman standing at the top of the stairs, looking first one way and then the other. Through the plate glass in the large front door, Lela could see out into the street where snow was beginning to fall slowly in thin white flakes. A man went by with his coat collar pulled up around his face; he walked along swiftly against the wind. The old woman looked out and shivered. Then she turned and began to walk slowly by the ladies' underwear counter and stopped, gazing absently at flimsy garments of pink and white.

"Just look at her!" Lela said. "She just makes me positively ill."

"Why don't you tell Mr. Thompson?" Grace asked. "I think he's over on the other side."

"Well, I just think I will," Lela said. "You don't know what that woman's up to."

"Go ahead," Grace said.

"You said Mr. Thompson is over on the other side?"

"He was a couple of minutes ago," Grace said.

It was bad enough, Lela thought, to have to go through a perfectly terrible day without any sales at all and then have

33

to put up with that old woman poking around all over the store. Lela stood for a moment watching the woman and then she turned and went to look for Mr. Thompson. He was in the men's furnishings, leaning up against a counter talking to George Spencer about the football game the Saturday before. When Lela came up, he stopped talking and smiled at her.

"What's up?" he said.

"Mr. Thompson, have you noticed that awful-looking woman that's running all over the store? She's been in here for just hours and hours, and Grace and I were talking about her and we've just about decided she's a shoplifter."

"Yeh?" Mr. Thompson said. "Where?" He frowned.

"I saw her, too," George Spencer said. "She's been walking around all over the store."

"She has, huh?" Mr. Thompson said. "You haven't seen her take anything, have you?"

"No, no, I haven't," Lela said. "But it's just that she's all over the place. Grace and I were talking about her and—"

"Where's she now?" Mr. Thompson asked.

"Over on the other side," Lela said. "Honestly, Mr. Thompson, she just about gave me the creeps the way she was walking all over the place."

"We have to be careful," Mr. Thompson said. "We can't afford to insult a customer."

"She isn't any customer," George Spencer said.

"Oh, no," Lela said. "She's no customer."

"Well," Mr. Thompson said. "Well, I'll have to see about this."

"She's been in here so *long*," Lela said. "She's just been in here for the longest time."

"It sure looks funny to me," George said. "I said something to Louie Kronmiller about it and he said she was just some old woman that came in to get out of the cold."

"Cold nothing!" Lela said. "What's she doing going all over the store the way she is?"

"Yeh, that's what I'd like to know," Mr. Thompson said.

"If she wants to get out of the cold, why doesn't she go home?" Lela asked.

"Those damn people get me sore," Mr. Thompson said suddenly. "Come in here and think they've got the run of the place. Just bum around all over. You'd think the store was a railroad station or something. They give me more damn trouble."

George Spencer nodded his head sympathetically. "It certainly doesn't give the store a very good name to have people like that running all over the place," he said.

"You said it, George," Mr. Thompson said. "Where is this old woman, anyway?"

"She's over on the other side," Lela said. "She was the last time I saw her, anyway."

"It gives the store a bad rep to have people like that running all over the place," George said.

"They seem to get the idea that this store is a railroad station or something," Mr. Thompson said. "How do they get that way, will you tell me?"

"Well, that's what I say, Mr. Thompson," Lela said.

"This store doesn't cater to that kind of trade," George said.

"Trade!" Lela said. "Trade! It'd be different if she'd buy something. But she doesn't have any money. Just poor trash, on relief probably, with nothing better to do than go running around stores all day."

"I'll show her she can't get by with that stuff around here," Mr. Thompson said. "Watch me."

Lela watched Mr. Thompson going over to the other side. The more she thought about it, the madder she got. It just made her boil. And she was beginning to get pretty irritated about Dale not calling her up. Lots of times he would call her up at the store during the morning. Not this one, though. Why didn't he call? She loved him so, and how did he repay her love? How?

Mr. Thompson was standing up near the front door talking to the woman. Heavens, she was a repulsive old thing! The woman wasn't even looking at him while he talked to her. Oh, she knew she had been doing the wrong thing, all right! Couldn't even look Mr. Thompson in the eye. Lela looked beyond them through the glass door to the street. It was snowing faster. Lela made up her mind that she would eat that noon at the Ethel-Doris Tearoom around the corner. They had awfully nice lunches there. She wished that Dale would be eating with her. She thought of him just every single minute of the day, and what thought did he give to her? Men only wanted one thing, that was all. Oh, he didn't appreciate her, not one bit. He didn't appreciate her half enough, and some day he'd be sorry. He'd be sorry, all right.

"Thompson's sure telling her, don't think he isn't," George said.

Lela nodded. She saw Mr. Thompson's head moving up and down jerkily as he talked to the woman. You could see that he was pretty darn mad. Well, who could blame him? And that awful woman didn't even look at Mr. Thompson; she just kept staring down at her feet. And then after a minute she turned and opened the door slowly. A blast of cold air blew in. Lela shivered.

Mr. Thompson came back with a big smile on his face.

"Well, that's the way to get rid of that kind," he said.

"What'd she say?" Lela asked.

"Nothing; nothing at all."

"Didn't she say anything at all?" George Spencer asked.

"Didn't say a thing," Mr. Thompson said. "I thought I might send her up and have her frisked to see if she'd taken anything, but I didn't want to ask any of the girls to dirty their hands on her."

"That was nice of you, Mr. Thompson," Lela said. "She just gave me the creeps."

"Well, she won't any more," Mr. Thompson said, laughing shortly. "She won't come in here again after what I told her."

"That's the only language people like that can understand," George said.

Lela felt a lot better now that the woman was out of the store, but for some reason or other she still didn't feel good. Maybe if she got a call from Dale, maybe that would fix things up.

"Well, thanks, Mr. Thompson," she said. "I guess I'll get back to the other side."

"Not at all," Mr. Thompson said, watching Lela's swaying hips. "Not at all."

Then he turned back to George Spencer and said, "Well, George, what was it you were saying about the backfield? You were saying something to me about the backfield when Lela came over."

III

George had time for a pretty interesting discussion of the game with Thompson before he looked back to the shoe department and saw a man sitting in one of the chairs. He rushed back to wait on the man, but he wanted a pair of overshoes. George told him politely that he'd find those down in the basement, in the shoe department down there.

He went back where the shelves were and lit a cigarette. It seemed like an awfully long morning. Time just seemed to drag when there wasn't much business. Well, it was always pretty slow this time of year, but never as bad as it had been lately. The big White Elephant Sale would be coming off the first of next month, and then they'd be plenty busy around the store.

He sat down on a box, thinking about Little Orphan Annie. That was one of the best comics going, exciting, and sort of real, too. George felt sorry for Daddy Warbucks: there he had built up a great business, a business to benefit humanity, and what happened to him? A bunch of radicals and malcontents had gone to work and stirred up trouble for him. Like month before last when that strike had been on at that shoe company and they hadn't been able to get those gold dancing slippers, those B7301 numbers. Well, people are strange and there's no two of us alike, George said to himself.

He yawned. Such a long morning. He wished some customer would come in, just to break up the monotony. It would be swell if someone like Mrs. Stoner would come in. That woman would come in and buy five or six pairs of shoes at once. She had an interesting foot, Mrs. Stoner. And she always knew just what she wanted. One of his best customers. The more he had like her, the better he liked it.

George stood up and finished his cigarette. Didn't taste so good this morning for some reason or other. Maybe he was coming down with a cold. Not very often he came down with a cold; he had a good strong constitution and could throw them off easily. Lot of sickness right now, though.

He guessed that he'd go up front and kid with Lela some more. That girl was sure built nice, and that green wool outfit she was wearing showed things off just all right. George didn't think much of that guy she went with: he was just a wise, stuck-up, college guy that thought he knew it all. Hardly dry behind the ears, George said to himself. He couldn't figure out what Lela saw in him.

George wondered what that story was that Lela was going to tell him. He hadn't heard a good story in a hell of a long time. She usually had some good ones. He looked up front, but Lela had a customer. Well, he didn't feel like sticking around the department the way things were going. Too dull. He decided he'd go downstairs and read the sports section. He hadn't taken time earlier.

Walking up front, he went by Lela and winked at her. He didn't expect her to wink back at him because she had a customer, but she nodded her head and smiled. Lela was all right. He walked down the stairs, humming a little. There was the sports page to read, and maybe he'd take the time to read "Things in Chesterton," that column a local fellow wrote. He was pretty clever, too. Now and then he got off some good cracks.

He wondered briefly where the old dame had gone when she had left the store. But hell, that was just one of those things that happened, and it sure wasn't any concern of his. Maybe she had been a shoplifter; Thompson should have had her frisked.

Oh, well, George thought. He walked through the bargain basement, wondering if there was enough anti-freeze in his car. He guessed there probably was.

He hurried along to the men's room, looking forward to reading the sports page. There was nothing he liked better than to read the sports page; that was one thing about him.

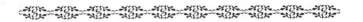

MRS. LUTZ

HOLDING THE MENUS in her puffy hands, Mrs. Lutz stared out of the window of the Ethel–Doris Tearoom. The sun was bright on the nickel-plated finishings of the Cadillac parked at the curb, and she moved slightly to get out of the reflection. From behind her came the sounds of dishes rattling and waitresses' steps in their flat-heeled shoes. Voices rose and fell in steady harsh waves.

What a fine day it was, and what a good crowd there was this noon, Mrs. Lutz mused. Every table filled but one. They were serving fresh strawberry shortcake, and the special was corn fritters with bacon strips. In a little while, she decided, she would go out in the kitchen and cut herself a nice little piece of that lovely cheese the chef had bought the other day. She had just finished her lunch an hour or so before, and a little piece of that cheese would be the very thing to finish it off.

Mrs. Lutz smoothed the white lace collar on her black dress and turned around, watching the waitresses to see if everything was going right.

She drew in her chin slightly. *Well!* Mildred had not given an ashtray to the man in the brown suit at Table No. 11. And there he was, forced to put his cigar ashes in his saucer, simply because of Mildred's negligence. That girl, Mrs. Lutz thought. I'll certainly have to speak to her about this.

She looked around the room, but Mildred seemed to be in the kitchen. Never around here when I want her. That girl! Well, Mrs. Lutz decided, she would just have to take an ashtray to the man herself. She'd just have to do it herself, she guessed. That was the way it went: If you wanted anything done you had to do it yourself.

She walked over to the cabinet and selected a metal one with a picture of a little black Scottie on it. She took it over to Table No. 11 and placed it on the tablecloth near the man's plate and said, "Here's an ashtray for you."

The man looked up absently and said, "Oh. Oh, thanks."

That Mildred, Mrs. Lutz thought, walking towards the front of the room. She kept an eye on the door to the kitchen, tapping her fingers impatiently on the menus.

Lucille came out carrying a tray and went over to Table No. 14. That was where Mr. and Mrs. Ledford were sitting. They were lovely people, the Ledfords. So devoted to each other. Good customers, too. They always liked to be seated at Table No. 14. It was their favorite table. Mrs. Lutz watched approvingly while Lucille removed the dishes from the tray and put them on the table.

A man in a gray suit got up from Table No. 3 and went over to the cash register to pay his bill. Mrs. Lutz smiled at him professionally, watching Eunice make change. The cash register said forty cents. The man had probably eaten the Busy Business Man's Special. It was forty cents, the Busy Business Man's Special.

The door to the kitchen opened and Mildred came out with a tray. Mrs. Lutz glared at her. About time you're showing up, young lady. About time you're putting in an appearance. Mrs. Lutz caught Mildred's eye and motioned to her to come over as soon as she got through serving the people at Table No. 8.

Mrs. Lutz walked over to Table No. 14, where the Ledfords were sitting. She smiled at them and said, "Everything all right today?"

"Just lovely, Mrs. Lutz," Mrs. Ledford said.

"Well, I'm glad of that," Mrs. Lutz said. She glanced in Mildred's direction.

"When are you going to have those apple dumplings again?" Mr. Ledford asked.

"Mr. Ledford is so fond of those," Mrs. Ledford said.

What fine customers they were, Mrs. Lutz thought. It was a pleasure to have people like the Ledfords for regular customers.

"About next Thursday, I think," she said. "About next Thursday."

"Mr. Ledford is just so fond of those dumplings," Mrs. Ledford said.

"Well, I think we'll be having those again next Thursday," Mrs. Lutz said. She would have to remember about that and speak to the chef. "They are good, aren't they?" She saw that Mildred was waiting for her. "Excuse me," she said.

She called Mildred off into the corner where she could speak to the girl. Mildred was always very neat, she thought, looking at her closely. That was one thing you could say for her. At least you could say that, if very little else. Mrs. Lutz pursed her lips before she spoke.

"Mildred, I wish you would be more careful about seeing that people get ashtrays when they are smoking," she said. "I think I spoke to you about that once before."

She distinctly remembered speaking to her about it before.

"I'm sorry, Mrs. Lutz," Mildred said. "What table was that?"

"Number eleven," Mrs. Lutz said. "The gentleman in the brown suit over there."

"I'm sorry, Mrs. Lutz," Mildred said. "I'll get him one right away."

Oh, will you, young lady? "There's no need of that now," Mrs. Lutz said. "*I* got one for him."

"Oh," Mildred said.

Oh, indeed! Mrs. Lutz looked sharply at the girl. "I don't want to have to speak to you again about this," she said.

"Yes, Mrs. Lutz."

"Very well, then." Mrs. Lutz nodded her head to dismiss Mildred. She walked back to the front of the tearoom and stood there, holding the menus. It was really a lovely little tearoom, much nicer than the one she and Ethel had managed over on Baker Street. Really got a better class of people here. She wished they could have as good a crowd as this every day. Well, she couldn't complain. They were doing all right by themselves. Doris Lutz knew when she had a good thing.

Looking out of the window at the cars going by, Mrs. Lutz decided that she would go to a movie that afternoon. Francis Lederer was at the Rivoli.

She turned around. The man at Table No. 11 was reaching in his pocket. He took out a coin and put it under the rim of his plate. Mrs. Lutz watched the man, wondering whether he had ever been in the tearoom before, or whether she had ever seen him somewhere else in the past. No, his face wasn't familiar, even though it had seemed so at first. She never forgot a face, that was one thing about her.

It looked very much as if it was a quarter tip he was leaving. A quarter tip, indeed! For that Mildred! Well, I should say not, Mrs. Lutz thought. A whole quarter for that girl? I pay her eight dollars a week, and she's mighty lucky to get that, let me tell you, as many girls out of work as there are. That man certainly must like to throw his money away.

She watched the man putting on his coat, and when he had gone up to the cash register, Mrs. Lutz walked over to the table and glanced around. Mildred was in the kitchen. She looked again, just to make sure, and then she picked up the coin deftly and dropped it into the pocket of her dress. It was a quarter. She had just known it was a quarter.

A quarter tip! For that Mildred! A dime would have been a great plenty.

Mrs. Lutz went up front to greet a young couple who were coming in. She smiled at them. "Two?" she said brightly.

Leading them back to Table No. 3, she felt the quarter in her pocket. That would pay for her movie that afternoon, she thought. The quarter would just take care of her movie that afternoon.

She pulled the chairs out from Table No. 3 for the young couple and handed them each a menu.

"Lovely day, isn't it?" Mrs. Lutz said.

LETTER FROM MAINE

I

HENRY APPLEGATE, SR., was sitting on the porch-swing shelling peas for his daughter-in-law Julia. It was a fine spring morning. The sunlight spread over Henry Applegate's thin shoulders, warming him, as he rocked back and forth in the old swing. Henry was thoroughly pleased with the weather and the pleasant squeak the chains on the swing made.

As he shelled the peas, he hummed softly to himself. From time to time he would break out with a few measures of loud and nasal song, when he could remember the words.

When the postman came up the walk to the Applegate house, Henry was singing "After the Ball" at the top of his voice. "After the Ball" was a number that Henry knew very well. It had come out the year Henry had been married. His wife had died six years ago that spring.

Matt Griggs, the postman, came up on the porch and stood looking at Henry for a moment. Henry was slightly deaf and did not hear Matt come up.

"That's a good old tune, Henry," said Matt.

Henry looked up quickly.

"Good Goddie, but you gave me a start," he said. "You liked to frighten the wits out of me, Matt."

"I sure didn't mean to, Henry," Matt said. "It's sure a great morning, ain't it?"

"They don't make 'em any better'n this one," Henry said. "This is really a *morning*."

"It sure is a great one," Matt said. "I ain't seen you setting out on the porch for a long time, Henry."

"I been a little under the weather here lately, Matt. My innurds have been acting up like a house afire." Henry picked up some of the loose peas in the bottom of the pan and put a few of them in his mouth.

"That's sure too bad," Matt said. "Somebody said that you hadn't been feeling up to snuff."

"Oh, I feel fine now," Henry said, chewing the peas with his gums. "It takes a morning like this to put a feller on his feet."

Matt leaned against one of the white posts on the porch. "Well, there's no two ways about that," he said.

"You ain't got a letter for me, have you?" asked Henry, winking. It was a standing joke between Matt and Henry, for Henry averaged about two letters a year.

"Wouldn't you be surprised if I did?" Matt said. "It just so happens that I have got a letter for you, Henry." He rummaged about in his leather pouch and took out an envelope. "For Mr. Henry P. Applegate, Sr., Weston, Nebraska," he read. "I guess that's you, ain't it, Henry?"

"Well, good Goddie, where'n the name of sin is it from, anyway?" Henry took the pan of peas from his lap and put it down at his side on the swing. "A letter for *me*, you say, Matt? Where is it come from?"

"I can't seem to make out the postmark, Henry," Matt said, squinting at the envelope. "It's kind of smeared up a little."

Henry stood up and walked shakily to where Matt was looking at the letter. Just then, Julia, Henry's daughter-in-law, pushed the screen door open and came out on the porch. She had been standing just inside the door listening to the men talking.

"Good morning, Mr. Griggs," she said to Matt. "Give the letter here to me, if you please. Perhaps I can make out where it's come from."

Henry frowned angrily, but he didn't say anything. He watched Matt surrender the letter to Julia, annoyed with Matt for giving it to her. It was *his* letter, wasn't it?

"Well," Julia said, "I guess your eyes aren't as good as mine are. This letter is from Bangor, Maine. That's a big lumber center."

"Give the letter here and let me open it up," said Henry peevishly. "It ain't your letter, Julia. It's seldom enough that I get any letters that you should be hanging onto it like it was yours."

Matt Griggs, not wishing to become involved in any family arguments, said good-bye hurriedly and left. He was sorry he had handed the letter over to Julia Applegate. She was always putting her nose into other people's affairs.

"My cousin, Ruby Potter, used to visit people in Bangor, Maine," Julia said, ignoring her father-in-law. "I've heard her speaking of visiting people there several different times."

Henry had almost lost his patience with Julia.

"Are you going to give me my letter, or ain't you?" he said. "Give it here, Julia, I want to see who it's come from."

"Oh, very well," she said, thrusting it out at him. "Take it and quit crying about it."

Julia turned to go back into the house, but she was curious about the letter, and she stopped, waiting for Henry to take it out of the envelope.

Henry was so nervous that he had some difficulty in opening it. It was hard for him to make his fingers operate the way he wanted them to. As he took the letter from the envelope, he made a noise with his mouth. It was a sound that he unconsciously made when he became excited.

"Don't make that noise, Father," Julia said sharply. "I don't know how many times I've told you that. It sounds perfectly awful."

"Sorry," Henry said. He had been unaware that he had done anything.

He unfolded the sheet of white paper and read:

PROSPERITY CLUB

IN GOD WE TRUST

Henry concealed his disappointment. He had hoped that it would be a personal letter with "Dear friend Henry" written at the top of it.

Under the heading was a list of six names and addresses, which he did not bother to read. The body of the letter read:

"This chain was started in hopes of bringing prosperity to you.

"Within (3) days, make (5) copies of this letter, leaving off the top name and address, and adding your own name and address at the bottom of the list and mail to five friends to whom you wish prosperity to come.

"In omitting the top name, send that person ten cents (10 cents) wrapped in paper as a prosperity donation.

"In turn, as your name leaves the top, you will receive 15,625 donations amounting to $1,562.50.

"Now is this not worth a dime to you?

"Have the faith your friend had, and this chain will not be broken.

"Follow instructions and watch the dimes roll in."

Henry looked at the last name on the list to see who had sent the letter to him. He read: "Alonzo G. Weeks, Box 89, Bangor, Maine."

"Who's it from, Father?" Julia asked. She had been standing impatiently in front of the door, waiting for Henry to finish reading the letter.

"What do you know, Julia?" said Henry. "This here letter is from Lon Weeks."

"From who?"

"Lon Weeks. I guess you don't remember him. He was before your time. He used to run a harness shop down on lower Main about forty-five years ago."

"Oh," Julia said. She came over to him and took the letter from his hand. "What did he have to say?"

"Go ahead and read it," Henry said. "It's some kind of chain business. It was darn nice of Lon to remember me."

Julia glanced over the letter hurriedly and handed it back to her father-in-law.

"I don't want you to have *anything* to do with this, Father," she said. "I haven't seen any of these before, but I read a piece in the paper about them. A man in Denver started them. It's just a graft, and I want you to stay out of it. I don't want you to get mixed up in anything like this."

"Now look here, Julia," Henry said, "Lon Weeks sent me this to send on, and I know Lon wouldn't be mixed up in anything that was shady. It's my letter, and I'm going to do as I want with it. I don't have to take orders from you all the time."

Henry went over to the swing and picked up the pan of peas and handed them to her.

"Here," he said.

"You haven't finished shelling all of them, Father."

"No, and I ain't going to."

Julia turned on her heel and went back into the house.

II

Sitting in the front room that evening before supper, Henry could hear his son and Julia talking in the kitchen. It was hard for him to catch all that they were saying; Julia had closed the kitchen door, and Henry could not hear very well anyway.

49

"Good Lord, Julia," his son Henry was saying, "if he wants to go in on this thing, let him do it. He gets little enough fun as it is."

"I don't care," Julia said, her voice rising. "I just don't approve of such things as that. I don't want him mixed up in it. I read a piece in the papers—"

"I talked to Father about it," Henry Jr. interrupted, "and he isn't counting on getting anything out of it. He feels that he has a duty toward Mr. Weeks. Father used to know him a long time ago."

"A penny saved is a penny earned," said Julia. "I don't approve of throwing dimes away every chance you get. They don't come that easy."

"Well, I'm the one that earns them, and I'm perfectly willing to give him one. He doesn't spend hardly a thing since you made him quit smoking."

"Good for him!" Henry Sr. mumbled to himself. "Julia don't need to think she can run a man my age all the time. No, sir!"

From the kitchen, Julia's voice rose harshly.

"Now look here, Henry Applegate! You know I don't approve of smoking, and don't you think for a minute I'm ever going to let any man smell up this house with filthy cigar smoke! That's where I put my foot down! As long as your father lives under this roof, there'll be no smoking going on! I think he goes downtown sometimes and smokes some place or other. I smelled it on him no less than a week ago."

"I bet you let him know about it, too," her husband said quietly.

"I certainly did!" Julia replied. "He doesn't need to think for a minute that he's going to get away with anything around this house!"

The door to the kitchen swung open noiselessly, and

Henry Sr. saw his son coming towards him. Henry Jr. came over to the couch and sat down beside his father. He patted him on the arm.

"Let's let the whole thing drop, Father," he said softly. "Julia is plenty worked up over this."

"She can hear you from here," his father said.

"No, she can't. Listen, you go down to the post office tomorrow morning and send those things from down there, and drop a little note to Mr. Weeks, if you want to. Here's fifty cents; that ought to take care of your postage and dime and everything."

"All right," his father said. He began to smile.

"Now for Lord's sake, don't say anything to Julia about this," Henry Jr. cautioned him. "She'd raise hell about it. Put the money in your pocket and just keep still about it, won't you?"

"Sure I will. You're a good son, Henry."

"All right. Don't let Julia catch on."

Just then Julia came into the dining room with some plates and silverware. She glanced at the men suspiciously and began to set the table. She made as much noise with the dishes as she could.

"She's mad as all get out," Henry Sr. whispered.

They ate the meal quickly, anxious to finish and escape Julia's angry looks. Julia said very little during supper except to ask her father-in-law if he couldn't be more careful about spilling food on his shirt-front.

After they had eaten their rice pudding, Julia stacked up the dishes and went across the alley to see Mrs. Harold Newton, a member of her card club. She slammed the back door loudly on her way out.

"Well, let's wash the dishes, Father," Henry Jr. said.

"Might as well as not. She's sure mad as all get out, there's no two ways about it."

"She'll get over it," his son said, putting the teakettle on the stove.

"If your mother hadda lived, there wouldn't be none of this sort of thing going on." The old man took a fresh dishtowel from a drawer and unfolded it. "That Julia has got a temper on her like nobody else. She wants to run everybody's business. She won't let nobody do what they want to."

"Clouding up a little," Henry Jr. said, looking out of the window.

III

It was still raining a little Sunday morning, and after breakfast, Henry, Sr., went out on the porch and sat for a while, thinking how nice it would be to have a smoke. Julia had been speaking to him hardly at all for the last three days, but Henry did not care very much; he had sent his letter off and fulfilled his duty to the Prosperity Club and Lon Weeks. Julia had not found out about it.

Henry was wondering whether a pipe or a cigar would taste best right then, when Julia came to the door and looked out at him.

"You better start getting ready for church," she said. "You're always so slow."

"I'll get there all right," Henry Sr. said. "I always do, don't I?" He started to say that he didn't see any sense in listening to a minister that didn't have sense enough to swing his arms when he walked, but Julia had gone inside the house somewhere.

Henry stood up and went inside, grumbling to himself about Julia and the shortcomings of the new minister and how draughty it was in the church.

At eleven o'clock he was standing on the steps of the porch waiting for Julia and his son. Three church-bells in the same block down the street began to ring simultaneously, and Henry shuddered at the great racket they made.

"That damn woman anyway," he muttered. "Who does she think she is?"

Julia and Henry Jr. came out of the house. Henry Jr. was carrying an umbrella, and he put it up as soon as Julia had the door locked.

"Pull up your tie, Father," Julia said. "It looks a fright. Then I guess we'll be all ready to go."

They went down the street silently, watching the other people on their way to worship, walking carefully to avoid the puddles on the sidewalk. The bells, one by one, ceased their noise, and in the distance the only ringing that could be heard was the Baptist Church bell, six blocks over on Sherrick Street. It was a pleasanter-sounding bell than the others, Henry Sr. thought.

The service was just beginning when the Applegates arrived. When Henry, Sr., saw the new minister, the Reverend Mr. Maddock, who had come to Weston from Joplin, Missouri, he began to scowl.

"Stop that frowning, Father!" Julia whispered as they settled down into their pew.

The choir, directed by Miss Doralee Thomsen, sang Mendelssohn's "But the Lord Is Mindful." Henry Sr. had to admit it was pretty good for *their* choir.

The Reverend Mr. Maddock, the Church Bulletin announced, would take as the subject for his morning sermon, "Gambling in a Mad World." This was preceded by the offertory.

Henry, Sr., had some change left over from the fifty cents his son had given him, and he thought it would be fun to put it in the collection plate. But when he thought of Julia's questions as to where he got the money, he passed the plate on without contributing.

The Reverend Mr. Maddock began his sermon by pointing out that horse racing, the operation of slot-machines, playing cards for money, shooting dice, and lotteries were all forms of gambling.

"What's all this got to do with the Bible?" Henry Sr. mumbled to himself. "The churches ain't like what they used to be any more."

"Be quiet!" Julia whispered angrily, although she had not heard what her father-in-law had said.

"And now," boomed the minister, "and now, a great wave of the rottenest and most depraved type of gambling is sweeping over this nation, ensnaring the greedy amongst us! In a comparatively short period of time – only a few days – this country has become maddened by a new form of gambling that some vicious individuals have thrust upon us.

"*You* know to what I am referring! I am talking about this great wave of chain letters that has descended upon us, taking many in its grip, arousing the rotten greed that men will not wash from their hearts, instilling visions of great and ill-gotten wealth in those who are bound to be disappointed, defrauding many and *possibly* making a small amount of tainted money for a few!

"I ask you to *think* of what you are doing before you enter into this Devil's Bargain; I ask you to *consider* what it actually means! Many ignorant persons will invest a dime or a quarter or a dollar in the hope that they will reap untold riches. But for every person that makes a hundred dollars out of this most dishonest form of gambling, there will be a thousand who will have parted with a dime. It is the lowest and most contemptible form of gambling that I have ever heard of, and I hope that none of *you* have been so base as to become involved in this racket – for that's what it is – nothing more than a rotten, corrupt racket that–"

The Reverend Mr. Maddock warmed to his subject and continued in the same vein for some thirty minutes.

"Let us pray," he said finally.

Julia was wearing the same smile that she always had at the end of a church service. Henry Sr. wanted to punch her in the face.

They were among the last ones out, for Julia insisted upon sitting far down in the front of the auditorium. As they neared the door, where the minister stood erect, shaking hands, Henry Sr. walked past him hurriedly without stopping to speak to him.

He waited at the bottom of the steps for Julia and his son. It was still raining a little. People were putting up their umbrellas again, looking at the sky and talking about the weather, wondering if there was going to be much more of the rain. One man said there had been half an inch of rainfall during the night; another said that he didn't think there was quite that much.

Julia and Henry Jr. were the last ones out of the church, except for old Mrs. Hutchinson, who always stopped to talk to the minister for at least ten minutes after every service. Henry Sr. fell into step with them. They walked for half a block before anyone said anything.

When Julia was sure that they could not be heard, she turned on the old man suddenly.

"I've *never* in my whole life been so mortified!" she said. "You deliberately ignored Reverend Maddock. You talked all through his fine sermon. You certainly made a spectacle of yourself."

An automobile drove by them slowly, and Julia did not speak again until it was past them. Henry Sr. had known that he was going to catch it, but he hadn't thought that Julia would be quite as angry as she was. He looked at his son pleadingly, but Henry Jr. was afraid to say anything that would anger Julia more.

"Well, I hope you're proud of yourself, *Master* Applegate," she said. "You ought to be pretty pleased with yourself after what you've done this Sunday. I don't know what Reverend Maddock is going to think. What do you have to say for yourself?"

"If a person can't stand being euchred out of a dime, he ain't so much," Henry Sr. said.

"What's that?" Julia snapped.

"A person oughta count on losing his dime if he sends it out. That minister's a blame fool."

"*That* will be just about enough out of you," Julia said. "I've never been quite so mortified by anyone in all my life. Well, Henry, do you have to use all that umbrella for yourself? You might hold it over this way for a change, if you *don't* mind."

"I'm sorry," her husband said.

IV

Henry Applegate Sr. had not counted on getting anything out of the Prosperity Club chain letters, but when he heard the report that a woman on the west side of town had received two fruit-jars full of dimes since she joined, he began to wonder if he would get any money or not. The letters, according to newspapers and gossip, were spreading all over the country. A man in Lincoln was rumored to have bought a new Chevrolet with the money he had received. Matt Griggs told him that they had noticed an increase in the mail at the post office.

Since Sunday, Julia had not spoken to her father-in-law. And when Henry Jr. was called to Chicago on business for the company he represented, his father could hardly bear to see him leave.

"I'll only be gone for three or four days, probably," Henry Jr. told him. "It won't be so bad as you think."

"She'll make my life a living Hades, you watch," his father said.

Henry Jr. left Thursday on the train. He wanted to drive, but Julia would not let him take the car for such a long trip. She wanted to use it the next Sunday to take Mr. and Mrs. Harold Newton to Lincoln to see Mrs. Newton's sister. The Newtons did not have a car.

After his son had left, Henry Sr. kept away from Julia as much as he could. At meals she watched him constantly to see that his table manners were all that they should be; the rest of the time she left him pretty much to himself. After the first day, he was so lonesome for someone to talk to that he would have almost welcomed conversation with Julia.

He began to think a good deal about the letters, speculating as to his chances of getting any dimes. There were a lot of things he would like to have; for instance, enough money to get himself a room of his own. He wouldn't have to take anything from Julia then, and could see Henry Jr. just as often. Or he might take a trip down to Oklahoma and see his daughter Laura, now Mrs. Fred Oettinger. He hadn't seen Laura for three years, since she had flatly refused to stay under the same roof with Julia again. Laura had written several times asking him to pay Fred and her a visit, but Julia would not let Henry Jr. spend that much money on a trip for his father.

Saturday morning Matt Griggs arrived later than usual. Henry Sr. was in the front yard pulling weeds when Matt hailed him.

"Well, guess what I got for you this morning, Henry?" Matt said.

Henry stood up and came over to Matt.

"Not so loud, Matt," he said. "You got some mail for me?"

Henry felt his heart beating rapidly.

"You bet your boots I have," Matt said. "I didn't know you was mixed up in this chain letter business, Henry."

"Sh-h-h! Not so loud, Matt. I don't want Julia to hear us out here." He wiped his stained hands on his trousers. "You know how she is."

"Sure, I know. Well, I got nine letters here for you, Henry, and I wouldn't be at all surprised if there wasn't dimes in all of 'em. What d'you think of that?"

Henry looked around at the house cautiously. Julia was not in sight.

"Good Goddie, Matt!" Henry said. "That's a fair profit, ain't it?" He looked at the house again. "I sure hope Julia don't see us out here like this. You better give me the letters before she gets wind of what's going on. I'd catch it for sure."

Matt handed him the envelopes and grinned.

"I sure hope you get a lot more of 'em, Henry," he said. "I'd like to see you get rich."

Henry stuck the envelopes inside his shirt. He was almost sure that Julia had come out on the porch and was watching him, but when he turned around, there was no one there.

"Listen, Matt," Henry said, "maybe you better keep my mail down there in the post office from now on. I can get it at the General Delivery window instead of here, can't I?"

"You bet you can, Henry. I'll fix it up right this noon. You can rest easy on that score. I know how it is."

"Not so loud, Matt, not so loud. Julia would skin me before you could say scat, if she knew 'bout this."

"You leave it to me, Henry. You can get your mail at General Delivery after this noon." He started off down the walk. "I sure hope you get a lot of them dimes, Henry."

"So do I, Matt."

Henry walked hurriedly back to the garage. Inside, he closed the door, and in the semi-darkness, opened the envelopes. There were nine dimes, all right. He held them in his hand, looking at them, trying to think of a good place to hide them. He found an old tin can that Henry Jr. kept nails in. He dumped the nails out into a little wooden box and dropped the dimes, one by one, into the bottom of the can. Then he stuffed some cotton waste into it and put it on a high shelf. He thought it would be pretty safe there.

V

Monday morning after breakfast, Henry Sr. went to the post office. Julia had sent him down to the Piggly-Wiggly for some groceries, and on the way back, he stopped for his mail.

"Quite a bit for you, Mr. Applegate," the man at the window said. "Anyway thirty letters."

There were too many of them to conceal in his shirt; so Henry walked down the first alley he came to and opened them. He put the dimes in his handkerchief and tied it so that the coins would not rattle. There were thirty-two of them. He walked home, humming quietly.

Henry Jr. had to stay in Chicago longer than he had expected. By the following Thursday, the day he was supposed to get back to Weston on the evening train, Henry Sr. had twenty-eight dollars and sixty cents in the tin can. He would have had twenty cents more, but two of the envelopes had been badly sealed, and the dimes had fallen out in the mail.

After supper Thursday, Henry Sr. told Julia that he thought he'd go down to the depot and meet his son. Julia wanted to get the dishes done so that she could go to Shirley Temple's new picture that was showing at the Isis Theatre. She told her father-in-law to run along to the depot if he wanted to.

The train was late, and when it finally did pull in, Henry Jr. was not on board. Henry Sr. was disappointed, and he wondered what had kept his son over this time. He stopped at the baggage room in the depot to see Cobe Merden, but Cobe had gone home to eat. Henry started back to the house feeling depressed and lonely; but the thought of the two hundred and eighty-six dimes cheered him, and by the time he was in sight of the house, he was feeling much better.

Julia was standing in the doorway when he came up the porch steps. In her hand she had the tin can that Henry Sr. had used to hold his dimes. When Henry saw her with it, he was so frightened that his knees began to shake. He stopped and stared at her, the sound of his breath becoming louder and louder.

"This is the last straw, Father," Julia said. "A friend of mine was kind enough to phone me and let me know that you'd been getting a lot of mail at the post office these last few days. I *thought* you'd been up to something. I've been wondering why you've been going out to the garage so much. So you were gloating over your dimes, were you? What do you have to say for yourself? Speak up!"

"Gimme my money, Julia," he said weakly.

"You don't think for a minute that I'm going to, do you? This money isn't yours. It doesn't belong to you."

"What are you going to do with it?" Henry asked.

"Never you mind what I'm going to do with it. That's my affair, not yours. And you go down to that post office tomorrow and tell them your mail is to come *here* in the future. Now you get upstairs and get to bed."

"You ain't going to give that money to the church, are you?"

"You never mind what I'm going to do with it," Julia said. "Stop your whining and get upstairs. I don't want to hear another word out of you."

Henry climbed the stairs haltingly. He stopped on the landing for a moment, looking back at Julia, who was standing in the hall, glaring at him. He should have known he couldn't get away with it, he thought.

In his room, he dropped to the lumpy bed and took off his shoes. His feet hurt him. He stretched out on the bed, cursing to himself. He knew what she'd do with the money. She'd spend it on herself, just like she'd spent his wife's life-insurance money. She'd probably get a new spring dress with the dimes, or make a down-payment on the Frigidaire she was always talking about buying. It would be just like her.

He could hear Julia moving about in the room below him, getting ready to go to the movie. Damn her anyway, what right did she have to take his dimes like that? They were his dimes, weren't they? What right did she have to take them away from him?

He heard the front door slam, and the screen door after it, and the sound of Julia's heels on the front porch. Henry rolled over on his stomach and began to cry softly.

"That damn woman," he said. "That damn Julia woman."

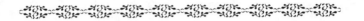

PUBLIC LIBRARY

Two dirty boys pushed around and around in the revolving door until one of the librarians came over and told them to stop at once.

I am not a fussbudget about what I read, but I do like a story that makes me feel uplifted when I've finished it.

On Wednesday, May 8th, the Library will present Mrs. Howard C. Wriston in a review of "Seven Grass Huts," by Cecile Hulse Matschat at Blucher Community Center.

Here is one you might like. It was made into a picture with Lionel Barrymore, and it has big type, too.

The man took a collapsible rubber cushion from his pocket, blew it up, screwed the cap of the valve on tightly, and put it on one of the chairs in the browsing room. He sat down and began to read *The Critique of Pure Reason.*

I'm a taxpayer and a property-owner and it seems mighty funny to me that I can't get a card just because I don't have any identification.

It is simply impossible to get the books I want here any more. This is the third time I've been in to get *Gone With the Wind.*

dear Liberian, please give Milton (little boy) two books by Kathleen Norris and Zane Gray (or other good cowboy book) to bring home. Thank you.

Mrs. Vernon.

No, I'm not going to leave a reserve card. I don't approve of them at all.

And there he was, back of one of the filing cases, cutting out pictures of nudes with a razor blade.

It is very strange that that book is not in.

On Wednesday, May 15th, the Library will present Miss Grace Gore Murchison in a review of "Night in Bombay," by Louis Bromfield at the Bode Branch Library.

Get a Bess Streeter Aldrich for Grandma.

I am positive that I asked the girl to stamp them for four weeks. I don't see how those books could be two weeks overdue.

Tell those boys to leave that revolving door alone!

I don't know the name of it, but it's a little green book with gold printing on the outside and my aunt had it out last Spring.

I imagine you people that work in the library have lots of time to read all the good new books.

Dear Librarian: Enclosed is an autographed copy of my book of poems, *Petals from a Bluebell*, which I am happy to present to the Library with my compliments.

> Sincerely,
>
> (Mrs.) Elizabeth Martin Winkelman.

The *Atlantic* is splendid this month, one of their best issues.

There was a drunk man back in the stacks who was annoying one of the patrons, but the janitor threw him out almost immediately.

I would like to get a book on religion someone was telling me about, but I don't know the title or the author's name.

Why must they write such books when there's so much that's unpleasant in the world already? That's what I'd like to know.

On Wednesday, May 22nd, the Library will present Mrs. Virgil B. Porter in a review of "Union Now," by Clarence Streit at Blucher Community Center.

Did you remember to buy the canary seed and the Kitchen Klenzer? You check your books out at that desk. They make you write your numbers now.

I have been going back and reading some of the older authors like F. Marion Crawford and find them very refreshing.

We representatives of Moral Rearmament have twice asked the Library to change the subject-heading in the catalogue from "Oxford Group" to "Moral Rearmament," but so far nothing at all has been done.

No, I don't care to read anything but historical novels and books about small-town life.

For Heaven's sake, leave this door alone!

There will be no book review on May 29th. Blucher Community Center is being used on that date for a symposium of "Whither America?" On the following Wednesday, however, Mrs. Harold O. Utterback will review "How to Read a Book," by Mortimer J. Adler.

THE LIBRARY

FOUR SKETCHES

1. Back Room & Front Desk

IT WAS SNOWING HARD that morning and the sky was gray. Miss Black had turned on the lights and glanced through the building. It was such bad weather that the only people in the library were a couple of old men in the periodical room who were looking at yesterday's newspapers.

Miss Black noticed the snow that had been tracked in on the tile floor, and she frowned and pressed her lips together firmly and went into the back room. She made no noise when she walked: her heels did not touch the floor.

The new girl was waiting for her. She was very thin and had large hazel eyes. When Miss Black came into the back room the girl was holding a book in her hand, leafing through it slowly. She raised her eyes and smiled at Miss Black.

Miss Black did not smile. "Miss Quade told you about your hours, didn't she?" Miss Black said.

"Yes, she did," the girl said. "She said –"

"Very well," Miss Black said. "That's all I wanted to know." She went to the long table by the window. It was covered with new books. "Here's what I want you to do right now," she said. "You know all about identification marks of course, Miss –"

"Zimmer," the girl said, coming over beside Miss Black. "Martha Zimmer."

"Oh yes.... As I was saying, do you know about this method of identification? The pin-hole?"

"I don't believe so, Miss Black. I don't understand just what you mean."

"Oh, I see," Miss Black said. "Well, now pay attention here." Miss Black picked up a red-covered book from the table and turned to page ten. Opening a drawer, she took out a pin. "This way. Just take a pin and stick it through the zero in the number ten." Miss Black perforated the zero with the pin. "Like that, you see. We always use it here as a method of identification, along with all the others. So many people stealing books. Now get right at it and go through all of these books, all in these five stacks."

"Well, I never heard of that before," Miss Zimmer said.

"Well." Miss Black rolled up the windowshades. It was snowing harder. The ground was white except for a few scattered places where the dead grass still showed through. "When you get through doing that, I'll show you around the building and see that you have something else to do," Miss Black said.

There was the sound of footsteps from the main room. Miss Black smoothed her dress and went out to the loan desk. There was a young woman in a brown coat leaning against the railing. There were flakes of wet snow on her coat and her hair.

"Yes?" Miss Black said.

"I haven't been able find the book I was looking for," the young woman said. "I looked in the stacks. I thought that perhaps it would be in the back room."

"Yes?" Miss Black said. "Just what is the title of the book you're looking for?"

"It's Lewis Corey's *The Decline of American Capitalism*," the young woman said. "I'm quite sure it's in the back room. I know that one of his books was."

Miss Black looked steadily at the young woman for a long time. Then she said, "Oh . . . . Well, just a minute." She turned and walked silently to the back room.

Miss Zimmer was going through the books, punching the zeros. When Miss Black stepped inside the door, the girl looked up and smiled and said, "Am I doing this all right, Miss Black?"

Miss Black did not answer her. She stared steadily out of the window at the falling snow, her face stiff. She was scarcely inside the door, and her hand was still on the brass knob. Miss Zimmer looked questioningly at her, her smile fading, but when Miss Black stared sharply at her, Miss Zimmer hurried on to another book and turned to page ten.

Miss Black turned suddenly and went back to the loan desk.

"That book is not in," Miss Black said.

"It isn't?" the young woman said. She frowned. "Why, that's strange."

"That book is not in," Miss Black said firmly.

"Well . . . all right," the young woman said. She stood uncertainly by the desk for a moment. "Well, thank you."

"Not at all," Miss Black said coldly.

Watching the young woman go back to the stacks, Miss Black stood at the desk stiffly. She cleared her throat and smiled tightly to herself.

II . Homage

The room was lighted by a forty-watt bulb in a lamp with a frayed rose-colored shade, from which strings of broken yellow beads dangled. The girl sat in a rocking chair below the lamp, the dim light pouring on her coarse hair. In the kitchen there were sounds of dishes rattling.

Staring through thick glasses at the book in her lap, the girl looked away for a moment to the wall, where a large calendar hung. There was a photograph of the Dionne Quintuplets in pink rompers; below the picture were the printed words: MOTHER MAYO'S FEMALE REMEDY "THOUSANDS THANK GOD FOR IT."

A girl put one of her fingers inside her thick lips and bit off a piece of fingernail and spit it out. She looked at the book again. Picking up a stub of pencil on the table beside her, she wrote on page 203 of the book: *If my name you wish to know, look on page* 239. She stared at what she had written, carefully dotting the *i* in *wish*.

Then she put another finger in her mouth and chewed on it, removing a sliver of fingernail and holding it between her thumb and index finger to examine it carefully. She wiped it against her skirt. She looked again at the calendar on the wall.

In the kitchen a woman sang in a cracked voice:

Jesus is waiting to save you
Open your heart to him now

and then the song died away into a mumble.

The girl turned to page 239 and wrote: *If my name you wish to know look on page* 285. Then she turned to that page and wrote: *If my name you wish to know, look on page* 304. And at the top of page 304 she printed carefully in large letters: HA! HA! FOOLED YOU!!

She smiled, and a giggling sound came from her throat. She looked at what she had written, her smile widening, and then she closed the book quickly and held it out from her. On the back was stamped *Leaves of Grass Walt Whitman*.

Someone moved in the kitchen: there were sounds of leather against wood, the squeal of a faucet being turned, and then the faint noise of a stream of water running and gurgling in the drain.

The girl opened the book again and turned to the title page and wrote: *This is a dirty filthy book. I hate it.* Then she raised one hand close to her eyes and stared at her fingernails, her face expressionless. She closed the book and went to a rack by the door and put on a greenish-black cloth coat and a black felt hat with a metal ornament on it that looked like a beetle.

"Mama!" she called. "Mama!"

A woman's voice came from the kitchen. "*What?* What is it? Don't scream so."

"Mama, I'm going to the library now," the girl said.

An old woman came into the room. In the dim light her skin seemed to be a faint yellow color. "You wait until your brother gets back," she said. "He'll be back 'fore long." She stood in the kitchen doorway, a dishtowel in her hand.

"Oh, Ma!" the girl said. "He won't be back for a long time yet."

"You heard what I said. You wait for your brother now. I don't like you going out on dark nights at all hours by your-self." She sniffed. "Funny smell in here."

The girl closed her hand over the doorknob. "I don't smell anything," she said.

The old woman sniffed again; her upper lip quivered. "Well, *I* do. *I* smell something."

"Oh, Mama, you're always smelling something."

"I know when I smell a bad smell," the old woman said. She hobbled about the room, sniffing noisily. "I've got a sharp nose on myself, and don't you forget it. I can smell things a dog can't even smell."

The girl followed the old woman with her eyes. She stood with one hand pulling at her skirt, the book under her arm. The clock whirred and struck once. The girl looked at it. The hands were pointing to seven-thirty.

"Oh, I can smell something, all right," the old woman said.

"Oh, Mama!"

"Ahh, here's what it is!" the old woman cried. "Here's what it is making that smell. This." She snatched at a corncob pipe that was on the table behind a vase. "Ugh! Smelly old thing."

"Tom he bought it the other day," the girl said. "He's breaking it in."

The old woman made a noise through her nose. "I'll break him in," she muttered. She looked up. "Well, what are you standing there for?" she asked suddenly. "Get along with you to the library if that's where it is you're going. Don't be standing around the house with your coat on just to catch your death of cold when you go out. Haven't got the sense of a field mouse, I do declare."

"Gee, I thought you wanted me to wait for Tom," the girl said.

"Oh, get along with you," the old woman said, putting the pipe in the pocket of her apron. "Get along with you before I lose all patience."

"All right, Mama," the girl said. "I won't be gone so long."

"You get back in a hurry. I don't want you dillydallying along."

"All right, Mama." The girl opened the door and went out in the hall. She put her ear to the door for a moment and then glanced around nervously and took a compact from her purse. The hall light reflected on her mirror-thick glasses. She held the compact close to her face and put on powder and rouge and lipstick. She made little noises to herself, smearing the red salve until it was thick on her lips. She grinned at her image reflected on the inside of the compact's cover. Then she clicked it shut and put it back in her purse and went outside and down the brick sidewalk, the *Leaves of Grass* clutched tight against her lumpy body.

III . All the Way There & All the Way Back

Like a corkscrew the stairway rose from the main floor behind the reserve desk and spiraled upward to end before a door with a sagging knob. The old man climbed the stairs slowly and stood at the top. He breathed heavily. He opened the door and went inside.

The room was small. The ceiling sloped to the window, and outside on the narrow stretch of roof between the window and the gutters there were pigeons cooing and strutting back and forth, their purple and white feathers dirty with coal soot.

The old man dropped to the single bed by the window and closed his eyes. He lay there motionless for some time, and after a while his breathing became even and effortless. The bed was unmade, and the twisted white sheets drooped almost to the floor where a single rag carpet lay. There was a sign on the wall: WHEN YOU GET TO THE END OF YOUR ROPE, TIE A KNOT IN IT AND HANG ON. And on the sign there was a picture of a man hanging on to the end of a fraying rope. There was a knot in the end of it, and the man appeared to be climbing the rope slowly, with great effort.

After a while the old man rose from the bed and stretched and went to the dresser and opened one of the top drawers. He took out a writing tablet with a picture of an Indian chief on the cover. He pawed around in the drawer and found a stub of pencil and then he went back to the bed and sat down and opened the notebook to a fresh sheet of the rough blue-lined paper. He touched the tip of pencil to his mouth and wet it and began to write. He wrote each word slowly.

Dear Son Tom: I was glad to get your letter of Aug. 21 and lern that you and Della and the "kids" are geting along beter now and you are all alright. that was sure a cute thing the litle fellow said, he must be geting to be a prety big boy by now. would sure like to see him and all of you. sure wish I coud come up and visit you on my "vacasion". but Tom I guess I shoud explain about that. I have never said nothing before to you or Della or nobody about the way things are here much. on acount of I dont want to wory you or Della none about me you got trubles enuf of your own. but here is the way the situation is, I am hired by the city as "custodian" for the library and my contract specifys that I am suposed to get 2 wks. off every year with pay. but this place here is so full of graft and corupsion that it dont work out that way. on account of the old woman who is librarian I don't dare to call my Soul my own. she is the menest woman God ever let draw breth and why He dont strike her dead is a mistery to me. on account of this situasion I dont hardley dare to call my Soul my own. and if I was to take a "vacasion" without no pay I would probably come back here and find another man in my place when I come back. so that is the way the situation is. the old woman who is the librarian is in "cahoots" with the library bord and others in the city govt. and they get away with murder. I canot proove it. but I no that I dont receive my full salry. so you see how the situation is with me. they make me live here in a litle dinky room that you coud not swing a cat in and I have to pay duble to the price of one like it in any place else. they also made me get rid of my Dog. well Tom maybe some day things will be different with me. but you see how it is now and why a "vacasion" is impossible for me to take ever as long as I am here at this place. well guess I must close now my eyes have been trubling me a lot latley and the "dr." tells me I beter rest them all I can or I wont have no eyes left at all. wrote to Ila the other week but have not herd from her as yet. well write again soon Tom, with love to you and Della and the "kids."

Your Father,
Wm. Mapes.

P.S. no I dont no where Sam Goodridge is now.

When he had finished writing the letter it was beginning to get dark. The sun was down. The old man stood up and went to the dresser and turned the bulb that hung from a pale green cord. Then he took an envelope from the drawer and addressed it and stuck a stamp on it. He went to the little closet in one corner of the room and put on his hat and coat.

He stood for a moment looking at the envelope, and then he put the letter inside. He licked the flap of the envelope and sealed it. Then he turned off the light and slowly felt his way down the twisting stairs.

IV. Miss Van Wie, Miss Quade, Miss Spangenburg

It was six minutes to eight when Miss Van Wie looked at the clock. She left the main desk where Miss Quade was checking in books and Miss Spangenburg was checking them out.

Miss Van Wie had very slender hips and long legs and light wavy hair and greenish-blue eyes. She went into the periodical room and hurried from table to table picking up magazines that people were no longer reading. Three or four men followed her with their eyes. One young man who was reading *Aero Digest* and who wore a red sweater with a white letter *M* on it nudged another fellow sitting next to him. The other fellow looked up questioningly from the copy of *Popular Science Monthly*, and when the one in the red sweater nodded toward Miss Van Wie and said, "Nice," both of them gazed at her, their eyes hard and bright.

Miss Van Wie paid no attention to any of the people in the periodical room, but went about her duties hurriedly, picking up the magazines and putting them back in their places on the racks. The last magazines she put away were *Time, Town and Country, Photoplay,* and *Business Week*. Then she left the room, her hips swaying slightly, and went in the back room and put on her hat and coat. She looked at herself in the mirror briefly before going out into the main hall again.

A young man in a dark suit was standing by the door, and when he saw her he smiled, and Miss Van Wie smiled back at him. She took his arm and said, "Right on time again.

Aren't you the dependable one, though?" And he looked at her and said, "You can always count on me, Elaine."

Miss Quade had just finished checking out three books on religion to a poorly-dressed man and she had nothing to do just then. She watched Miss Van Wie going down the steps holding on to the young man's arm. Miss Quade wore the same expression watching the young couple as she had when checking out the books on religion to the poorly-dressed man.

Miss Quade took off her glasses and the slender gold chain rolled up: the glasses dangled from the round gold fob on Miss Quade's dress. Miss Van Wie and the young man were out of sight. The door still swung faintly behind them.

Miss Quade turned to Miss Spangenburg. There was no one at her side of the desk just then, either. Miss Quade went over to Miss Spangenburg and said, "Well, I see that Harris person picked up Elaine again."

Miss Spangenburg looked up from the reserve cards she was checking through and said, "What? What did you say?"

"I say: that Harris person stopped for Elaine again this evening. He was waiting for her."

"Oh, is that right?" Miss Spangenburg asked. She kept on with her work.

Miss Quade frowned. "You know what they say about *him*," she said.

"No, I don't. What do they say?" Miss Spangenburg said without interest.

"Why, everybody knows about him."

"Well, I've never heard anything. I'm sure Elaine knows what she's doing." Miss Spangenburg sorted out a pile of cards and tapped them on the desk, straightening them.

"Hmmm," Miss Quade said. "Well, that young lady had better watch her step around here in the future, that's all."

"Well, for goodness' sake!" Miss Spangenburg said. "What's the matter now?"

"Oh, nothing," Miss Quade said mysteriously. "Nothing at all. She'd just better watch her step, that's all I have to say."

Miss Spangenburg didn't speak.

"She'd just better watch her step," Miss Quade went on. "You mark my words."

"I don't know what you're talking about," Miss Spangenburg said.

"I was talking to Miss Black the other day," Miss Quade said. She paused for a moment. "And I think that young lady had better be mighty careful, that's all."

A man was standing on Miss Quade's side of the desk with some books to be checked out. Miss Quade turned and went back to her work, flipping the books open and stamping them JE 17.

When Miss Quade had gone, Miss Spangenburg stood for a long time with her eyes fixed on the reserve cards clutched in her hands. She bit her lower lip and picked up a pencil and began to make some sort of mark on one of the cards, but she was pressing too hard and the point broke. Miss Spangenburg stared at the little end of lead that had broken off the pencil, and then after a moment she brushed it off the desk. It made no noise at all as it dropped on the floor.

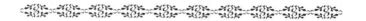

THE EVENING OF
THE FOURTH OF JULY

THERE WERE EXPLOSIONS everywhere. McGoin decided that it was impossible for him to concentrate any longer on the Bhagavadgita, which he had been trying to read. Putting the book down, he dressed and left his room. On the porch, he unrolled the newspaper to see what was happening in the world. Deaths and injuries from the holiday celebrations had exceeded the wildest prophecies, he noticed. He briefly scanned the headlines. A notorious Continental pervert was being feted in New York. A captain of industry predicted better times and announced a thirty-five percent wage cut. There was a picture of him making the announcement. He had a flower in his buttonhole. A ravishingly beautiful Hollywood star was to undergo a dangerous rectal operation at Mother of Christ Memorial Hospital. There were brief accounts of various murders, rapes, swindles, divorces, wars, poisonings, accidents, and beatings, and an illustrated feature story of an interesting child-torture case, in which the torturer claimed to have employed his razor blades and red-hot irons to bring a consciousness of Divine love to his youthful victims.

Explosion after explosion followed. One looked for the buildings to topple over, to see passersby clutch at their hearts and fall over into the street. The effects of the day's celebration were wherever one looked: the street, caught in the light of the burned-out sunset, resembled some thoroughfare in Hell. It was littered with red fragments of fire-crackers, strips of paper flags; bunting; broken cardboard horns, blown with such zeal throughout the morning that they were useless by the middle of the afternoon, paper hats of red, white and blue; crumpled cellophane; empty pop and beer bottles; and a ripped picture of George Washington, on which someone had drawn a crude Vandyke and horn-rimmed glasses. Across the street, a shaggy and bloated dog was chewing with tired persistence on what appeared to be a human arm.

In the front window of the drab brown house from which McGoin had come were a Rooms for Rent sign, with the "s" reversed, and a potted fern that had not been watered for some time. The fern seemed like the whole city at the end of the day, exhausted and hot and dying. Its leaves at the edges that rubbed against the dirty windowpane were crisp and brown.

Letting the paper drop, McGoin stood for a moment and surveyed the street. The only person in sight was the little man in the derby hat. McGoin has seen him many times before, and he accepted his presence as inevitable. The derby, green with age, seemed a symbol of both heat and punishment.

Except for a somewhat sinister gaze, which vanished when he became hilarious, the little man resembled those unfortunate figures in newspaper cartoons of the Average Man. As McGoin came down the steps, the man removed his derby and slowly wiped his forehead with a white handkerchief. It occurred to McGoin that this might be a signal, and he searched the street for another person who might be the little man's colleague. But there was no one except for a fat little girl on the corner, uninvitingly scratching her pelvis.

From all over the city the explosions continued with a persistence that seemed to come only from desperation. From several blocks away, near the viaduct, there was a noise like a machine gun. The harsh crackle of a spit-devil sounded from the rear of the house where he lived.

The little man had sneaked up on him. "Going somewhere, eh?" he asked. This observation evidently gave him considerable amusement, for immediately he was doubled up with laughter. McGoin watched him in astonishment.

"That's a good one, that is," the man continued, grinning and looking McGoin in the face. He had no teeth. His gums were purple as though he had been eating berry pie.

"What's good about it?" said McGoin.

The little man stopped laughing. As his smile faded, straightening his wrinkles, he said solemnly, "This is a great day. A very great day. Don't you think so?"

"No. Quit hanging around. You're getting to be a pest."

This brought on another unreasonable fit of hilarity. McGoin walked away. Once he looked back, and the little man was disguising himself by putting on a false beard which he drew from his pocket. It was a very long white beard, somewhat motheaten, with hooks that fitted over his ears.

McGoin walked on slowly. He was still exhausted from his unsuccessful attempt to sleep. For some months he had been employed as a night watchman in a factory that manufactured gas masks. He went to work at midnight, relieving an old man who had an early shift, and got off at eight in the morning. McGoin made the rounds of the factory every hour with the aid of a flashlight, carrying a leather container over his shoulder which held the timeclock. He punched in at the boxes attached to the walls. The factory was always quiet and still, and the sounds of his footsteps echoed and re-echoed through the empty building. Now and then a train whistled by. These sounds filled him with a contented feeling of loneliness. The finished gas masks lay in small piles on long narrow tables. They stared at him through the darkness with their flat glass eyes.

Sleep had been difficult. The parade had continued for hours during the morning. Once he had angrily got out of bed to look out. A troop of teenage girls in khaki uniforms was passing. There were hundreds of these girls. They wore no makeup, and each carried a bayonet that glistened blindingly in the early sun. Their faces were intent and pleased, with the knowledge that they were being watched. One girl, whose tight khaki blouse could not conceal the bouncing of her breasts, carried a large placard that read: BUTCHER OUR ENEMIES! McGoin had gone back to bed, the steady marching noises rising and falling in persistent waves. A military band went by.

Then there had been the noise of fireworks throughout the afternoon. When he was able to sleep, he had had nightmares. Finally, around four o'clock, he had arisen and prepared a meal in his room. He had warmed up some beans and a chunk of beef, and he drank several cups of coffee. A small piece of the beef had lodged between his teeth. This was now giving him a good deal of trouble.

Passing a white house with several dirty children on the porch, he saw one of them notice his approach, put a lighted match to a mammoth cracker, and hurl it at him. He leaped just in time. Its explosion tore off a portion of the heel of his right shoe. He yelled threateningly at the children, who were somewhat unhappy at the slightness of the damage, and was immediately reviled by a white-haired old lady in a neat black dress, who was strolling past.

"I'd think you'd have some consideration for the innocent pleasures of tiny children on such a happy holiday!" she cried angrily. When he stared at her, appalled, she commenced to beat him over the head with her umbrella. This action helped to restore delight to the children on the porch.

McGoin escaped as quickly as he could, but not before the woman had bruised him rather badly. Several men came out of their houses and cursed him for annoying a harmless old lady. One of them had a rope. McGoin slunk down an alley and crossed to another street.

It was a depressing section of the city. He passed a café, small and dingy, where the window announced in peeling letters: *Melody Café "Where Harmony Rules."* The proprietor, a fat Greek in a damp shirt, was quarrelling with a washed-out blonde. As McGoin went by, they were shouting in loud voices of each other's mediocrity in bed.

The damage to his shoe was not so great as he had expected. He found that he could walk quite easily. The difference was scarcely noticeable. However, the powder burn on his heel was beginning to seem rather painful.

The streetlights came on. The sky was a slate grey, blending into a dirty orange in the west. McGoin approached a building where some emaciated men were picketing, wondering why they remained at so late an hour. Across the street, on a platform constructed of planks, a man in a wing collar and a black coat, giving the appearance of a figure in a temperance drawing, was haranguing an audience composed, evidently, of persons who had shot off their firecrackers. McGoin paused for a moment, next to a housewife who gave off an aroma of garlic, to listen to the man.

It appeared that he actually formed coherent words as he screamed into the several microphones, but the sounds that came from the amplifier were like the gutteral grunts and groans made by moving-picture Indians. The microphones, strangely, were ear-shaped, painted flesh-color; and the amplifier was a huge mouth with thick purple lips. McGoin looked about at the crowd, wondering what held them to this recital of gibberish. They did not appear in the least puzzled or disturbed, however; they seemed, in fact, entranced by the noises that came from the appalling mouth.

"Good horse sense," the garlic woman said.

Suddenly the pickets, ignored by the audience, were surprised by the appearance of a corps of uniformed men who leaped from a car that had noiselessly sped up. These men drew revolvers and shot the pickets quickly, in a businesslike way, without ceremony. The pickets, all five of them, crumpled like broken paper sacks of water. One of the men turned as he went down, a look of complete astonishment passing over his face before he fell limply, his head hanging over the curb above a pile of leaves and cigarette ends. A thin line of blood trickled from the corner of his mouth and dripped monotonously on the leaves.

All of this was accomplished with such speed that no one except McGoin seemed to have observed the slaughter. The sounds from the amplifier were so loud that the revolver shots were scarcely distinguishable from the explosions of firecrackers. The uniformed men briskly returned to their automobile, which had no license plates, and drove off.

McGoin tried to cry out, to call attention to what had happened, but the garlic woman nudged him savagely in the ribs and whispered in a hoarse voice, "Pipe down, you! Some of us want to hear what he's saying!" And a man on his left, who resembled a retired boxing-star, looked at him narrowly. "Trying to start something, eh buddy?" he asked. "Troublemaker, huh?"

McGoin left directly. The garlic woman gave him a hard look as he pushed his way out of the crowd. He headed for Vifquain's. He knew that his friends would be there.

He saw no one that he recognized at the bar, but in a back booth Jane Ellen Krubb was drinking with a group of persons, all of whom wore green turtleneck sweaters. As he went by the rows of booths, his eyes on Jane Ellen's red hair, Engblom grabbed him by the arm.

"Greetings!" Engblom said. "You see Schultheiss?"

"No."

"He was supposed to show up."

"Who's here?"

"Oh, Jane Ellen's back there, and Quayhagen's around. Most of the others left. There's Jackson, in the next booth."

McGoin regarded Jackson. Jackson sat by himself, looking moodily at the wood from which the booth was constructed. He was studying the formation of the grain in the wood. Jackson was a great disciple of a certain author whose philosophy was based on internal discipline and a contempt for crying out or protesting, no matter how much pain one might be called upon to endure. At the moment, Jackson had crabs. This was his present burden. He had got the crabs from a Negress who lived on the other side of town. He sat there, not saying anything.

"Jackson has the crabs," said Engblom.

"I know."

"Takes it well, doesn't he?"

Quayhagen came up. He was wearing a bow tie. He was a tall man with bushy yellow hair and bulging eyes.

McGoin anticipated Quayhagen's first remarks. He knew that he would sit down, press his arm warmly, and inquire if McGoin wanted to hear something very revealing about someone. He always did that. Quayhagen annoyed McGoin, and he was in no mood for him this evening particularly. Quayhagen's eyes bulged so that McGoin was afraid they might fall out.

"How are you?" Quayhagen asked, warmly pressing his arm as he sat down next to him.

"Do you care?"

Quayhagen's eyes bulged. "Do you want to hear something very revealing about Marcus Schultheiss?"

"No."

"You couldn't loan me five, could you, Vernon?"

"Absolutely not."

"I just thought I'd ask. Don't you want to hear this about Schultheiss?"

"I'd prefer not to."

The waitress had come over to their booth and was looking down at them murderously.

"Bring me a glass of whiskey, please," said McGoin. "A large glass."

"Well," Quayhagen said, "a couple nights ago Schultheiss was painting an abstraction and I was drinking bay rum and talking, you know, and –"

"Pardon me," said Engblom. He got up and went back to talk to Jane Ellen and the people in the green sweaters.

Quayhagen watched him for a long while, his eyes bulging with sadness. Then he turned to McGoin and said, "You know, I don't think that Engblom likes me very much. Do you?"

"I really couldn't say," said McGoin. He drank half of the whiskey.

"You know, Vernon, my wife has a lot of integrity," Quayhagen observed.

"Are you living with her again?"

"She left me Thursday. That makes the sixth time. Couldn't you loan me a few dollars, Vernon? I'll pay it right back."

"You still owe me twelve."

Quayhagen affected an expression of astonishment. "Twelve? Is it that much? It's inconceivable." He quickly changed the subject. "You know," he said, "I just came from the Wilkinson speech at the auditorium. A great crowd, and lots of enthusiasm. Let me tell you, Vernon, it gave one a good deal of confidence."

"Yes?"

There was a mild explosion from outside. Engblom returned as though synchronizing his appearance with the noise. Just behind him was the little man, disguised as a

Spanish dancer. He wore a pink shawl and there was a rose behind his ear. He stared fixedly at McGoin for a moment and then went to the back exit, where he took a notebook from his pocket and made some notes in it. Then he went out.

"I was just telling Vernon about the speech," Quayhagen said to Engblom. "Wilkinson gave a magnificent account of our history, didn't he, Engblom?"

Engblom studied the glass in his hand. "Yes. A history of war and murder and poverty, decline and greed, frameups and disease."

"Magnificent!" exclaimed Quayhagen, his eyes quivering dangerously far out of their sockets.

"Wilkinson concluded on a note of hope," said Engblom.

The waitress came over at this point in the conversation and sponged the table listlessly and went away. Quayhagen kept his eyes on her. "A fine girl," he observed. "She reminds me of my wife, somehow. By the way, Vernon, do you want to know something very revealing about my wife? She is a lineal descendant of Thomas à Kempis."

This revelation seemed to produce an effect upon Engblom, for he stood up and went back to talk to Jane Ellen again.

"Do you want to get in on a good thing?" Quayhagen asked McGoin tensely. It was necessary for him to repeat his question in a somewhat louder tone, for a particularly loud explosion sounded, frightening a woman driver to such an extent that she ran onto the sidewalk, striking and killing a party of young people on their way home from a Campfire Girl's meeting.

"Do you want to get in on a good thing?"

"I'm in on one already. The great match swindle."

"Vernon, you're one of the only people I can talk to anymore. Do you know that?"

"I hadn't."

"It's true. What kind of an existence do you think I have to look forward to? Night after night after night? The loneliness—"

"Are you still taking cocaine?"

Quayhagen made no reply. They turned to watch Jackson rise and walk erectly between the rows of booths. He was scratching himself furtively. At the slot machine he paused, inserted a coin, and pulled the lever. Three lemons came up. The nickels poured out of the machine.

"Jackson is lucky tonight!" Quayhagen exclaimed. He stood up. "Pardon me, Vernon. Perhaps Jackson will be so kind as to loan me a little."

Engblom came back to the booth. With him was a woman who wore a flowered dress of a hideous green color and a hat shaped like an inverted chamber pot. The hat had a long purple feather sticking from it that served to emphasize the dumpiness of her figure. She wore the enrapt, pleased, and stupid expression common to some of the women in Rousseau's family paintings. Her face was puffy and eager, and she fixed McGoin with a gleaming eye.

"Vernon, I'd like to introduce Miss Ridpath," said Engblom. Engblom made a habit of digging up such people. "This is Mr. McGoin," he went on. "Miss Ridpath is very active in local Adult Education circles."

"Delighted to meet you, Mr. McGoin," she said rapidly. She had a high nasal voice. "Do you think that I might get a cup of hot tea here? What do you think of the recent statistics released by the Institute of Books in the Home? I regard it as a challenge to all of us, every one. I love the classics. If we are going to remedy the appalling situation which has come to light through the fine work of the I.B.H., we cannot take it lying down."

Jane Ellen Krubb had just come in time to catch Miss Ridpath's last remark. "Do you know a better way to take it?" Jane Ellen asked with a pleasant leer.

Miss Ridpath examined her with annoyance mixed with uncertainty. Pursing her lips she turned away, trying to attract the attention of the waitress. She still wanted a cup of tea. But the waitress was busy with her own affairs. She was being dated up by Quayhagen, who had borrowed, from Jackson, a dollar and a half in nickels.

"Have any of you seen Schultheiss this evening?" Jane Ellen asked. "Oh, hello, Vernon dear!" she exclaimed, her eyes growing large. "How are you?"

"I can't complain."

"You darling. You mean you won't. Are you still working in that horrid foundry?"

"It's a factory."

"Oh yes! I knew it was something like that.... You haven't seen Schultheiss at all? I don't know what in the name of God he's done with himself. Vernon, why don't you and I do something later?"

"Perhaps we could."

"We might do something."

"I have to go to work before midnight."

"That horrid foundry! Why don't you get a job in the day-time?" She examined her nails briefly. "Well, I've got to go back and see what my new friends are doing. They're trapeze artists." She waved at McGoin as she walked away. She had bright red hair. Watching the smooth way her body moved, McGoin wondered if her hair was dyed.

"Who was that person?" Miss Ridpath asked irritably. She had finally managed to get the waitress, ordered a cup of tea, and had been brought, instead, a powerful beverage, three-fourths alcohol, that was a favorite of stevedores.

"Oh, just a friend of ours," said Engblom. "Now, what was it you were saying about the I.C.H.?"

"The I.B.H., Mr. Engblom," said Miss Ridpath. "Fortifications or Food?" she went on. "Union Now or Destruction Later? What Does National Woodwork Week Mean to American Youth? Is Birth Control Patriotic? Can We Stay Out? Hear Lillian Bladderwort Gunzel Discuss 'After John Dewey – What?' next Wednesday at Murphy Community Centre.... What do you think of Socialism, Mr. – what was the name?"

"Moomaw," said McGoin. "I had it changed though."

"Spengler!" Miss Ridpath said, with sudden inspiration. "Spengler is such fun! Don't you agree with me thoroughly, Mr. Moomaw?"

"Oh, definitely."

"Is the Public Library a People's University? James Joyce – Genius or Charlatan? Is the Church a Living Force? Bombs or Bread – Can We Have Both? Human Values. Education by Radio. The nation is seething with enthusiasm for such topics!"

She rose, unable to contain herself, tremendously enthused, her face flushed; and as she did so, a trap door beneath her sprang suddenly open. She dropped, the rush of air blowing up her skirts, revealing a slogan embroidered in bright blue letters on her pink bloomers. FORWARD WITH ADULT EDUCATION! they read.

Several drunks, observing Miss Ridpath's spectacular disappearance and thinking the floor show had already begun, applauded and whistled approvingly through their teeth.

Engblom and McGoin watched the trap door close.

"A challenging figure, Miss Ridpath," said Engblom, taking a long drink from the glass the waitress had brought for her.

"Don't let them kid you," Engblom was saying.

McGoin and Jackson were listening to him. McGoin, now and then, would attempt to remove the piece of meat from between his teeth, but it would not come out.

87

"The nations do not want war," Engblom went on, glancing disapprovingly at McGoin's actions. "Poverty is being erased. Cutthroat politics, double-dealing, hypocrisy, executions – all things of the past. A spirit of tolerance and brotherhood grows on every hand. Look at the situation right here in this country. I think we have much to be thankful for. Little tots growing up with a new understanding of the nature and mysteries of Life. People with a real desire to make themselves whole, to turn themselves into great men like Leonardo da Vinci and William Jennings Bryan."

Engblom had been going on in this way for some time. A half hour had passed since Miss Ridpath's unfortunate accident.

A woman in heavy makeup led her small daughter, dressed in a cheesecloth ballet costume, to a clearing in the room, where the little girl stood nervously, her skinny knees knocking together. Accompanied by a harmonica which her mother drew from her reticule and blew upon wheezily, she played several trombone solos, selections from Wagner, all rather loud for the size of the room. During this entertainment, a bitter-looking man with bags under his eyes circulated a petition protesting a recent action of the mayor. The action, whatever it was, was not stated with sufficient clarity for anyone to know what it was they were protesting. Everyone signed, however, the drunker patrons of Vifquain's taking advantage of the occasion to practice their penmanship. One of the customers, who was at the point of unconsciousness, became very unpleasant when the man circulating the petition objected to his using it for the "around and around" and "up and down" exercises of the Palmer Method.

McGoin left during the free-for-all that developed. Tiny sputterings of small firecrackers mingled with the larger explosions. Streams of colored sparks unrolled through the mottled dark sky. The moon shone sourly. He was surprised to find Jane Ellen waiting for him behind the wheel of her roadster. He was even more surprised when the little man emerged from the shadows and opened the car door for him. He had substituted for his Spanish dancer disguise the simplicity of bushy red sideburns and a huge artificial nose. McGoin got in the car, and the man closed the door.

"Anything I can do," he said, going off into a fit of laughter that caused his nose to wobble. "Anything at all!"

"Who is that odious little person?" Jane Ellen asked as they sped through streets of pawnshops, second-hand clothing stores, broken barricades, and gutters piled with the drunk and injured.

"He keeps following me around. I don't know who he is."

"I'd certainly put a stop to it," Jane Ellen said, turning the corner at sixty-five.

"Where are we going?"

"I don't know. Don't you like just to ride and ride, with the night wind blowing through your hair?"

"Let's go up to your place."

"No, we shouldn't, Vernon."

"Why not?"

"You know what happens when I'm alone with a man."

"That's what I had in mind."

"Really, we oughtn't to.... Which way shall I drive back?"

They returned by way of the shore drive. Someone was shooting off fireworks on a boat far out on the water: plumes of sparks, yellow and pink and white, hung in the sky for a moment, reflected in the ocean. An airplane went by overhead, dropping blue bombs that exploded just before they struck the water.

"Beautiful, isn't it?" said Jane Ellen. "I just can't understand what became of Schultheiss this evening. I couldn't reach him anywhere."

Jane Ellen's apartment was at the top of a three-story building overlooking the ocean. It had once served as a boot-

89

legger's hideout. She parked the car on the beach and they walked over the sand, the small waves breaking behind them.

"We'll have to be quiet," she informed him as they went inside. "The people downstairs have Bright's disease."
Later, he watched the ceiling as it caught the lights reflected on the water. Far off, out on the ocean, a whistle sounded and died mournfully.

"I've got to go," McGoin said. "I wonder what time it is."

"Stay all night, honey. Say you will."

"I've got to go to work."

"It must be all spooky and strange at night, isn't it? All those machines. Don't you ever get scared?"

"No."

"I'd get scared. I know I would. I saw a movie once and a man was trapped in a factory all night and couldn't get out. Expressionist photography."

"Did you notice what I did with my necktie?"

"That French actor was in it. He's such a darling."

McGoin had found his tie. Through the window he could see the tails of skyrockets, green and orange and white. A faint booming came from the other side of town. Some children stood in the street below and waved sparklers in rapid circles; the light caught their pale smiling faces.

"How long has it been since you've seen Schultheiss?" Jane Ellen asked.

"I couldn't say."

"He was here last night. It's funny: Schultheiss looks like that actor, the one that was trapped in the warehouse."

"I thought you said it was a factory. You never get anything right."

"Darling, is this any way to talk to me after I've been so nice to you? I guess it was a warehouse. Schultheiss is such a darling. I think I'm in love with him."

"You don't say?" said McGoin. With his fingernail, he picked at the piece of meat between his teeth. It was caught very firmly. He would have to get something that would take it out.

He talked to her for a few moments more and then he felt his way down the dark stairs. The Bright's disease people downstairs were pounding on something. It was cool outside. He walked along the shore until he came to Waldemar Street, where he stopped at a drugstore to buy a spool of dental floss. Two of the toughest-looking men he had ever seen were lounging on the corner as he came out. "I'm troubled by these recurring rumors of athlete's foot at the West Side Y.M.C.A.," one of them said softly.

McGoin walked toward his house, turning the spool of dental floss in his pocket. It was reassuring to know that Jane Ellen was really a genuine redhead. It was something that had bothered him for a long time. Now there was no possible doubt.

The celebrations were almost over. The explosions had practically ceased. A whiskey bottle was thrown at him from a passing automobile, but he ducked and heard it crash into a store window behind him.

The car circled the block and returned to try it again with another bottle. McGoin was caught off his guard; the blow of the second bottle stunned him somewhat, and he leaned against a tree to recover. The pain made him forget the powder burn on his heel.

He opened his eyes and saw that the little man was standing in front of him. He no longer wore a disguise.

"You want to come with me and celebrate?" the little man asked.

"No."

"This is the greatest holiday in the year. You better come."

"Go away, for God's sake."

"See what I got in my hand?"

"A flag."

"You betcha. *The* flag. It's a flag with many precious associations. Think of all the many heroes its folds have covered in death! And the many that have lived and died for it!"

"Yes," said McGoin. He held a hand to his throbbing head and tried to leave, but the little man was too quick for him.

"Where do you think you're going, buddy? Nobody can treat the flag like that. This is the greatest flag that's ever waved o'er the home of the brave and the land of the free. Wherever this grand old flag has gone, it's been the herald of a better day. Know what I mean? Do you sigh for the triumph of truth and righteousness?"

"No," said McGoin. "Not any more."

"You ought to sigh for the triumph of truth and righteousness," the little man admonished, a bottle falling from his pocket. "The flag's got three colors. Know what I mean? White is the symbol of purity."

"Like your dear old mother."

"That's right. And it symbolizes the purity and incorruptness of our statesmen, and the honesty of our businessmen."

"And the purity of our dear old mothers."

"Yes, yes," the little man said rather impatiently. "In fact, it stands for everything that is Godly. And the red stands for love. It comes from the color of blood, and serves as a constant reminder that every true patriot should be willing to die for the love of country and shed his lifeblood in the hour of the nation's peril. Isn't it a glorious banner? Aren't you proud that it keeps alive the glorious traditions of our forefathers?"

McGoin broke away. The man was shouting a patriotic poem by Annie Chambers Ketchum, waving the flag and weaving blindly in the street.

McGoin pushed through a crowd that was examining the remains of several small boys who had been throwing containers of nitroglycerin at each other. A young man persisted in pushing after him. He had a brakeman's haircut, a bad breath, and an alarming case of acne, and he was clumsily trying to pick McGoin's pocket. McGoin eluded him and went on. Once, when he glanced back at the dark street, he saw that the little man had a cripple by the lapel of his coat. The cripple was trying to beat him off with one of his crutches.

McGoin went to his room. During his absence, the house next door had burned to the ground. An hour remained before he had to go to the factory. He hated the thought of going there; the eyes of the gas masks seemed to appear in his own room. Fireworks portraits of Herbert Hoover, Will Rogers, and Elbert Hubbard shone through the leaves of the park trees. McGoin stood at the window and looked out. The little man, beaten insensible by the frightened cripple, lay in a pool of light below. In his hand was the small flag he had been waving.

After McGoin had removed the piece of meat from his tooth, he went to bed and stretched out. He picked up the Bhagavadgita. What an excellent volume it was! It gave one much food for thought. He could read for at least half an hour; then he would have to go to work.

The Bhagavadgita was even superior to the Koran, which he had finished the week before. He was nearly through with the Bhagavadgita. Perhaps he could finish it this evening. He was eager to get on to something else. Listening to the sound of the house across the street falling in, he decided to start in on Bulfinch's Mythology later in the week. That was a good one, everyone said. He had heard nothing but laudatory statements about Bulfinch's Mythology.

THE BROTHERS

MYRON ANDERSON was still angry when he came home from the studio. Riding home on the streetcar, he found it difficult to get his brother out of his mind. It was the fourth time Joe had failed to make the broadcast, and it had taken all the smooth talking Myron was capable of to pacify the higher-ups at the radio station. Joe would have an excuse, though, he thought. He always had an excuse. He could be depended upon to have one all worked out.

He got off the car at Xantha Street and walked three blocks to where they lived. The two brothers were still holding on to the house, and they had a couple of roomers. Their mother had died several months before and left the house to them, along with a first mortgage. They were waiting for an agent to find a buyer.

Climbing the steps, he picked up the evening paper and looked in the mailbox, but there wasn't anything. It was dark in the front room and he turned on the light, considering what he would say to his brother when he showed up. If he did show up, he thought. From time to time, Joe would stage twenty-four-hour disappearances.

The goldfish were swimming lethargically in the bowl by the window. Myron took some fish food from a box and scattered it on the surface of the water. He watched the fish swim up to the white flakes and nibble at them. He liked watching them. It had originally been his brother's job, feeding the goldfish, but Joe had experienced the greatest difficulty in performing this task; and after one of the smaller fish had died and the others began to look slightly ill, Myron took over the feeding. Their mother was responsible for the fish. She had got them, along with the bowl, at a drugstore. They were a premium for buying more toothpaste than the three of them could probably use in a couple of years. There was still some of it left when she died.

The house was still and empty. Myron would be glad when the agent found a buyer and they would be able to move into a small apartment. He went upstairs and took off his shoes and stretched out on the bed for a while to read the paper, but after a few minutes he turned off the light over the bed.

He lay in the darkness, resting his eyes and listening to the ticking of the clock. The light that came in the window was gray and smoky and he looked out at the roof across the alley, remembering previous scenes he had had with his brother. Once, when he had overheard some dirty remarks Joe had made about a girl Myron knew, he had called him about it, and there had been a fine scene. Then there was the time when Joe had been in a jam over a stolen car. It had been a good one, too. Another time, they were going to kick him out of high school for cheating. It was also a good one. There had been a lot of good ones.

He knew it was Joe when he heard the doorknob turn downstairs, even before he heard his footsteps. Joe opened the door more quietly than either of the two roomers, turning the knob quietly and surely, with the technique of sneaking in that he had developed when he was in high school, coming in drunk late at night from basketball games. He closed the door and Myron listened to him walking through the house and up the stairs.

"Oh, hello," Joe said, coming into the room. "You home?" He looked about cautiously in the semi-darkness, wearing a false smile and not looking quite straight at his brother.

"Yeh, I'm home. I'm quite a homebody, as a matter of fact."

"Reading, eh?"

"Just trying to see if there was anything in the paper about you. Where the hell have you been keeping yourself?"

"I thought that's the attitude you'd take."

"Oh, for God's sake," Myron said.

"Every time it's the same way. Every time you jump to conclusions. You act like a goddamned protecting angel. You always think it's my fault. I'd have got there if I could." He was looking at himself in the mirror.

"What happened this time?" Myron asked.

"I don't really know if it's any of your business."

"Oh, you don't really know? Listen Joe, I wish you could have been there to hear the excuses I made for you at the studio. Or maybe you don't want to hold that job. Maybe you think you can find easier jobs than that. If there are any, I'd certainly like to hear about them. Two hours a day. When you manage to show up, I mean. Two hours. You don't really know whether it's any of my business, eh? Well, that certainly is fine. All right, maybe it isn't my business. I don't know. Maybe I ought to let them can you. Maybe that would give you a little sense. I doubt it. I goddamned well doubt it."

"You're in a grand mood, aren't you?"

"Perfect," said Myron. "On top of the world." He lit a cigarette. "Come on, I'm waiting for your story. Blonde?"

"Accident."

"Another one? What are you trying to do? Establish a record?"

"I was with Jack."

"Who?"

"Jack Wilkie. We were in his car and he ran through a closed street sign and then into a tree."

"A closed street sign. What won't they put in his way next? That must have been very nice."

"Could I help it?" Joe said. "What do you want me to do? The cops came and took us down to the station and I got locked up as a witness. Jack was pretty drunk."

"What a lot of splendid friends you have. I suppose you were leading the temperance forces yourself."

"I'd had a couple. Jesus, Myron, I couldn't get to the phone or anything. They had me trapped there. Those dumb bastards wouldn't even let me use the phone. You don't know how I argued with those guys." Joe became animated. " 'I've got to report to the studio!' I said. 'I may lose my job!' A hell of a lot of good that did. They just laughed at me and told me to take it easy."

Myron looked up at the ceiling.

"Was it my fault?" Joe went on. "A thing like that could happen to anybody. Could I help it that I was with him when he had to pull a stunt like that? Christ, there wasn't anything for me to do."

"You might try running around with more inhibited types than Wilkie for a change. Or did that ever occur to you?"

Joe was looking at himself in the mirror again. He had a scratch on his cheek and his left hand was bandaged.

"Why do you have to run around with nuts like that?" said Myron.

"I don't know."

"You sure did get us into a nice little fix this afternoon."

"I'm sorry as the devil, Myron. Honest." His voice had a repentant tone.

"Now listen, Joe, Mitchell almost went through the roof today, and this is the second time in three weeks. I had to talk like the devil to keep your job for you."

"It sure won't happen again."

"That's what you said before."

"I mean it this time."

Joe went in the bathroom. It was very dark in the bedroom and Myron sat up, feeling numb. He began to get the feeling that always came over him after such conversations. He would think of his mother and remember the way she talked to him about Joe and how she had always told him to look out for him. Myron was the older one, and his mother had never allowed him to forget it.

The two of them were acting in a radio serial. Myron had got the job for his brother after Joe had been unable to hold three other jobs. The name of the serial was *The Adventures of Uncle Herb.* Myron took the title role. He loathed Uncle Herb. He felt that Uncle Herb was undoubtedly the most odious old character that he had ever come across. The whole program was beneath him.

Because of his close association with the program, he had come to regard it as the most ghastly thing ever produced by a radio station. Its followers had no such criticism to make. No matter how banal and insipid the episode, no matter how much fun some of the actors privately made of it, letters would pour into the studio, many of them asking Uncle Herb to solve their various problems, domestic, economic, and erotic; and the sales of K–O, the product which the serial advertised, were mounting steadily. K–O was a very popular beverage which Myron, from curiosity and a misguided sense of duty to his sponsors, had once sampled. It had tasted like embalming fluid.

In each episode of the serial, which went on every afternoon at five o'clock, except Sunday, lasting for a half-hour, Uncle Herb and other rural characters, lovably portrayed, would become involved in all manner of seemingly overwhelming difficulties. These were always neatly straightened out in the last few minutes by Uncle Herb, who spoke haltingly through his nose.

Myron sat on the edge of the bed thinking about Uncle Herb and his brother and about the house and why the hell they couldn't get a decent price for it, and then he put on his shoes and combed his hair and called to Joe to ask him if he wanted to go downtown to eat with him.

"You go ahead, Myron," Joe said behind the door. "I've sort of got a date."

"All right."

"I'll see you later."

"Rehearsal tomorrow morning," Myron said.

"Don't worry. I'll be there."

"Try to make it on time for once."

He could hear Joe splashing in the tub. "You don't need to worry about me," he said. "From now on I'm the Punctuality Kid."

"So long," Myron said. Everything went along wonderfully for several weeks. It was too good for Myron to believe. Joe was on time for all rehearsals and broadcasts, and he even seemed to take more interest in his diction, which Myron felt had never been more than adequate. The biggest change was in his drinking. He quit altogether.

Once, riding down to work on the streetcar, he confided to Myron that he was seriously thinking of saving his money and attempting to go back to college. It would mean four whole years for him. He had had one year at the State University, where he had distinguished himself by passing in only two subjects, American History and Physical Education. Myron had come to the conclusion that the passing grade in the history course was an error of the instructor.

But Joe's model behavior did not continue for long. Several nights later, after they had come home and collaborated on cooking the dinner, Myron began to feel sick. He had had a similar attack several months before and the doctor had given him a prescription that had fixed him up very shortly. The medicine was all gone but Myron found the prescription among some papers in the desk. He told Joe that he was going to bed and asked him if he would mind going down to the drugstore to get the prescription filled.

"Do you have to have it right away?"

"Go ahead, Joe, take it down for me. You don't have anything else to do right away, do you?"

"What's the rush?"

"I want to get that stuff in my system and try to get some sleep as soon as I can. Wait a minute, I'll give you some money."

"You'd better. I'm broke."

"Saving it up to go to college?"

"I gave that idea up. It didn't seem worth while."

All Myron had was a ten dollar bill, and he gave it to him, cautioning him to be careful with it. "That's got to last until the first of the month."

"I'll be careful with it," said Joe. He seemed rather put out because he had to run the errand.

Myron went upstairs and took a bath and went to bed. The symptoms seemed to be worse than they were before. Perhaps, he thought, they weren't the same symptoms. He went through all the diseases he might be getting, feeling worse with the thought of each disease that occurred to him and debating whether or not to call the doctor. His body was breaking out in a rash.

An hour went by. Joe did not come back. Myron got out of bed and called the drugstore. He felt feverish. Joe had not put in an appearance there at all, they said. Myron was unable to tell them about the medicine, because Joe had the prescription.

When he began to have intermittent attacks of chills and fever, he rang the doctor. He came over immediately. When Myron told him that there was no-one in the house to take care of him, the doctor looked him over glumly and announced that he must go to a hospital at once. He had scarlet fever. They took him in an ambulance to the hospital and shot him full of serum. He was unconscious most of the night.

He almost died. It was several weeks before he was sure where he was. He stayed in the hospital for several weeks, losing about a pound a day; and the studio would send over letters that had come in from Uncle Herb admirers. Everyone was wondering about Uncle Herb and asking when he would be back. Myron was too sick to care. Sometimes he would wake up in the night and wonder why he wasn't dead.

As his health improved, Myron speculated on what kind of a story the studio was giving out about him. Uncle Herb was being played by another man at the station whose real gifts lay in the realm of the negro dialect; but Myron did not feel sufficiently interested to ask for a radio to hear how the character of Uncle Herb was being interpreted. He thought it would be rather nice if his successor gave Uncle Herb an Old Black Joe flavor. The doctor was very cagey about telling him how soon he might be able to return to work.

The day before they moved him back to the house, he read about Joe in the afternoon paper. He had been in another automobile accident. It was on the front page. It was his friend Wilkie again. It was Wilkie's last accident. He had been killed instantly. The car he had been driving had collided with two other cars on a crossing, and a girl that had been with them had been badly injured. Her name was Maxine Burgess. Her age was given as nineteen.

The steering-post had been rammed clear through Wilkie and, according to the account in the paper, the girl would be crippled and might very conceivably lose the sight of one eye. Joe had escaped with a few minor injuries. The three of them had been in the front seat, with the girl in the middle, and from what the paper said, Myron gathered that Joe had only been scratched and bruised a little.

There was a picture of Wilkie's car, or what remained of it, on the front page; and inside, of course, another editorial on safe driving, inspired by the accident. There was also a blurred picture of the Burgess girl, taken when she was in junior high school. She wore a middie blouse in the picture.

They took Myron home the next day. He sat in the car with the interne, looking out at the streets. When they went up to the house and opened the door, there was Joe.

"Well, welcome home," he said grandly. "The sick man's well again."

"Get out of the way," said Myron. He thanked the interne, who seemed embarrassed and asked him if he would be all right. "I'll be all right," Myron said. The interne went down the steps and back to the car.

With the exception of a piece of court-plaster across his forehead, Joe looked perfectly whole. He was dressed to go out, wearing a top-coat and a dark gray hat Myron had never seen before. The hat did not seem to go with the rest of him.

"What's your grouch?" Joe said. "Still sore at me?"

"Yes. Will you kindly get the hell out of here?"

"Listen, Myron," he said, "I know you think I'm three kinds of a bastard...."

"That's right. You're three kinds of a bastard. So now that you've got it all figured out perfectly, I wish you'd clear out."

"That night you were sick..."

"I don't want to hear about it. I don't want to hear any more of your goddamned phony excuses. You'd let the gold-fish die. You'd let your brother die. You'd let your own mother die if she hadn't beaten you to it. And it's a damned good thing she's dead, too. Goddamned good. Do you get that?" Myron was shouting. He was very thin and pale. "Now for God's sake get out of here, will you? I don't like to look at you."

"Listen, Myron . . ."

Myron started upstairs. He had lost eighteen or twenty pounds and was very weak. He held on to the bannister, trying to get his breath.

"Listen, Myron," Joe was saying, "I got a buyer for the house."

"All right, sell it," Myron said. "Get a lawyer and I'll talk to him. Sell the house, do anything you want; but stay away from me. I'll be out of here in a day or two. I'm going to get a room."

"I'd certainly hate to have your temper."

"Oh, for Christ's sake, get out of my sight."

"Don't worry about that."

"Have you managed to hold your job at the station?"

Joe felt of the patch on his forehead, wetting his lips. "They canned me. Today."

"I don't wonder. That a new hat you've got? It doesn't look right."

"What's the matter with it?"

"It just doesn't look right."

"It belonged to Wilkie," Joe said. "He was wearing it – you know, night before last, when we had the accident."

"So now he's dead and you're wearing it."

"It's funny; it wasn't hurt a bit," said Joe. He took off the hat and examined it with admiration. "Why shouldn't I wear it?" he asked. "I was his best friend, wasn't I?"

"Goodbye," said Myron, going upstairs.

In his room he lay down on the bed. The climb had winded him. He heard a horn honking outside and Joe going down the walk. Then he heard the car drive away.

It was chilly in the room and he noticed that someone had been using it during his absence. There was an empty gin bottle on the dresser and a pair of dirty socks in one corner. Whoever the visitor was, he had left some cigarette burns on the window-sill.

Myron looked down at his clothes. They were much too big for him now. He felt terribly tired, but he was gradually getting his breath. The doctor had told him that he could probably go back to work on Thursday. That was three days. He would call the station before long and tell them.

On Thursday he would take the streetcar to the studio and walk through the waiting room where people with piano-accordion cases would be sitting with blank expressions on their faces and where the new announcer with the wasp waist and the waxed mustache would be talking in a voice that was not yet completely free of a Kansas accent, and Myron would wait with the others in the ante-room while the Studio Ramblers completed their rambling, and then another Uncle Herb episode would be on the air.

Myron tried his voice on some of Uncle Herb's stock remarks, to make sure that he had it under control. It was fine. There wasn't a flaw. The lack of practice had not destroyed his Uncle Herb technique in the least. He pulled a blanket over his legs, feeling very tired. It was pleasant to know that everything was going to go smoothly from then on.

"It'll be all right now," he thought, clumsily pulling at the blanket.

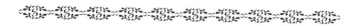

DO YOU LIKE THE MOUNTAINS?

IT WAS BEGINNING to get dark in the room. The two men sat in large green chairs by the window and looked out at Vine Street. Neither of them lived in the apartment, which was rented by three acquaintances of theirs – a stand-in for an actor at Warner Brothers, an extra who had not worked for several months, and another young man whose family gave him a liberal allowance to stay away from Sacramento. All of them were out at the moment. Across the street, a man was changing the letters on the marquee of the theatre and people went in and out of the vegetarian restaurant.

"I was out there on the desert for thirty-eight days, drawing twenty-five a day," Bryan said. He was a very tan young man who wore a white sweater, gray flannels, and rope-soled shoes. "Most of the time we just laid around and played cards and drank beer. Wonderful food. Then on the thirty-eighth day, Morgan decided to shoot the scene I was in. I rode up on a big white horse, my hair all mussed up, so dirty my own mother wouldn't have recognized me. Just as I get up to Braggioni – he was the heavy – I fall off the horse, panting like hell. They put a camera right over me and shoot from above and I say, 'They're on their way now, Stockton. Get out while you've –' Just that, see? Then I break off and fall over, a stiff. Twenty-five a day! The first take was good and the next day I came back to Hollywood and sat on my tail for six months before my agent found anything for me."

Magriel looked at his watch and said, "Let's go over there if we're going." He was younger and had not been in Hollywood long enough to have as good a tan as Bryan's.

They took the elevator down. There was a tall red-bearded man in the elevator who had a parrot in a cage. The lobby was empty except for a dwarf playing the pinball game in the corner. They got Bryan's car at the garage and drove up Vine to Hollywood, where they turned off to the left.

"You'll like Jimmy," Bryan said. "That guy has been just like a father to me. Always thinking of the little things. Always remembers my birthday, things like that. He and my father were awfully thick. Maybe he can give you some tips. He knows everybody." Bryan turned off the ignition as they coasted into a curving driveway.

An individual who resembled a retired pugilist opened the door for them and grinned loosely. "You ain't been around for some time, Mr. Bryan."

"San Francisco."

"What were you doing up there, Mr. Bryan?"

"I was in a play."

"How was business?"

"Not bad. Jimmy around?"

"He's taking a shower. Go on down to the bar and I'll tell him you're here."

Magriel followed Bryan downstairs. It was the longest bar he had ever seen. Behind it was a mirror that extended the length of the bar, and above the mirror was a mammoth painting of a very pink nude being ogled by a satyr.

"Been away, haven't you, Mr. Bryan?" the bartender said, wiping off the counter in front of them.

Bryan nodded. "You're looking fine, David."

"Never felt better. Been out of town?"

"Yes."

They gave him their orders. At the other end of the bar

stood two men, talking and looking at their images in the mirror. Their faces seemed familiar to Magriel.

"You recognize those two?" Bryan said.

Magriel nodded. They were two comedians who had been moderately successful before the advent of sound. He remembered the tall, thin-faced one in tweeds particularly well, although he seemed to have aged unduly. He had been splendid with the custard pies in the silent days. The other, a short, dour man with a spotty complexion, had dyed hair. Magriel didn't remember what he had been good at.

"They're always down here every time I come in, reminiscing about the old days or trying to figure out how to make a killing on the horses. Bert is pretty funny on the reminiscences when he's drunk enough. Trouble is, it takes an awful lot to get him that way these days."

He turned around. "Here's Jimmy now. How are you, Jim?"

Jimmy Farquar was a well-built man of about forty, conservatively dressed. He had a good tan and his eyes squinted slightly. He shook hands with Magriel, looking him over appraisingly, as though sizing up a candidate for a job.

"I guess I forgot to tell you that Jimmy manages the club here," Bryan said.

"Mr. Bryan," the bartender said. "Telephone."

When Bryan had gone to the other end of the room, Jimmy Farquar continued to look at Magriel, still holding his hand. "Like to see the place? I'll show you around if you'd like."

"Good enough," said Magriel.

"I'm going to show your friend around," Farquar called.

"Go ahead," said Bryan. "I'll just stay here and see how tight I can get before dinner."

They left him telephoning and went upstairs. Jimmy Farquar showed Magriel the lounge, an immense room with hundreds of photographs of actors on the walls. He pointed to several of them and recalled incidents of their subjects' lives. They walked around the room, looking at the pictures and the stone fireplace. On their way up to the second floor, they passed a famous leading man in evening clothes. He was quite drunk and did not reply to Jimmy Farquar's greeting.

Walking down the dark hall, Jimmy said, "Has Bob ever got a load on tonight? Come in my room a minute while I get a handkerchief."

The room was richly furnished, with a tiger-skin rug on the floor. The tiger's mouth was open and one of his teeth was missing. Magriel sat on the bed and looked out of the window at the lights on the hills while Jimmy Farquar got a handkerchief from the dresser.

"Never saw Bob as drunk as he was tonight. He could hardly make it down the stairs. He lives here now, you know. Broke up with Tanya last month. Well, offhand I'd say it was the smartest thing he ever did."

"Beautiful woman, though."

"You honestly mean that? Did you ever see her?"

"Not in the flesh."

Jimmy Farquar rubbed a finger across his forehead. "Up here," he said, "a big scar. She's growing a double chin. Her hair's six different shades from being dyed so much. There are only about two angles they can shoot her from any more. She sags any way you look at her. And temper! No, I mean it, the smartest thing Bob ever did was to split up with her. There was no happiness for him there." He went to the window and closed the Venetian blinds a little too casually.

"Known Bryan long?" he asked.

"No, not long."

"Great boy, Bryan."

"Yes," Magriel said. He was looking at a photograph on the dresser of a young man with curly hair and dark eyes.

"That's Billy French," Farquar said. "He was a wonderful boy. Died about a year ago. He was drowned swimming one night up the coast a ways. Got a cramp, the poor kid. I'm sure he would have had a big future out here. They were very much interested in him at Metro." Jimmy Farquar moistened his lips. "Yes, Billy and I used to go up to my place in the mountains and have wonderful times together. That mountain air is marvellous. I simply have to get away from here every so often, can't stand all the strain and noise. I guess I wasn't made to be a city man. Billy and I used to go up on weekends every chance we got and just lay around outdoors in the raw, soaking up a lot of that marvelous sunshine."

Magriel lit a cigarette and studied the picture of Billy French. He felt strangely uncomfortable.

"Are you working?" Jimmy Farquar asked.

"No. Not yet."

"You are an actor, aren't you?"

"Yes."

"I thought you were. How old are you?"

"Twenty-five."

"You look younger than that, you know."

"So they tell me."

"Probably not meeting the right people. This business of getting work, I mean. And you won't meet them through Bryan. I don't mean that the way it sounds – I've known Bryan since he was a baby, but he's lazy and he's thrown away all kinds of chances. Maybe there'll be some people at dinner tonight I can introduce you to. Would you like that?"

"My agent keeps saying it's only a matter of time."

"Oh, agents!" said Jimmy Farquar with contempt. He turned and picked up a cornflower from the dresser and put it in his buttonhole. "Do you like the mountains?" he asked.

"Not much."

"Really?"

"My nose bleeds," Magriel said, getting up. He did not like being alone with Jimmy Farquar. "Every time I get very high up I get a nosebleed. Hell of a thing, isn't it? Shall we see what Bryan is up to?"

Farquar studied him in silence for several moments. "If you like," he said. Turning, he glanced at his reflection in the mirror and smoothed his hair. "It's too bad you don't like the mountains. I was sort of thinking about going up this weekend."

He turned off the lights in the room and they walked downstairs. Jimmy Farquar nodded to a man in dark glasses who had just come in.

"Poor Billy French," Farquar said, as they descended to the bar. "You probably think it's silly, but there isn't a day goes by that I don't think of him a dozen times. The cramp hit him all of a sudden and nobody could get to him soon enough. It'll be just a year a week from Thursday." He removed a piece of thread from Magriel's sleeve. "It's a shame you can't go up to the mountains with me. You'll think it over, though, won't you?"

"I'll think it over."

"We'd have a fine time up there," Jimmy Farquar said.

Bryan was sitting at a table reading the *Reporter*. He looked up at them, grinning. One of the ex-comedians was playing *Liza* on the piano, badly, and the other comedian was discussing horses with a man who had come in.

Jimmy Farquar motioned to the bartender. "And now we'll have a little drink, and then I think I can promise you a remarkably good dinner." He smiled and felt of the cornflower. "You don't know how glad I am that the two of you could come over. There's so little real friendship in Hollywood these days. Well, I suppose there never was very much. You have no idea, Bryan, how lonesome I get. Not many people around any more like your father." His eyes settled on Magriel and he let them rest there. "Scotch and soda for you, Mr. Magriel? What is your first name? I feel like a fool calling you Mr. Magriel."

"Eric."

"Eric. That's a good name. Eric Magriel." He wore a thoughtful look. "Scotch and soda, Eric? Sure that's what you want? Bryan? Good enough. Two scotch and sodas, David. Just some dry sherry for me."

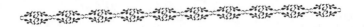

THE SIGN

WHEN MISS QUIVEY first came to work at the Public Library she noticed immediately that a great many things were wrong. Miss Quivey had worked in other libraries where, she felt, her experience had given her a valuable background; so it irked her to see all of the wrong things and not to be in a position to do something about them. She would sit at one of the desks, checking out books or taking them in or registering new patrons, dreaming of the sort of library she would have when she was a person of authority. In her mind, her own library grew, perfect and beautiful, and she saw things happening flawlessly under her skillful direction.

But Miss Quivey knew her place. She knew how persons of authority in any library resented criticism from a new staff member; and so the suggestions she made were usually of a minor nature. She would plan her campaigns for bringing up these suggestions with great care, and when she approached Miss Counselman or Miss Ambrosic or Miss Gates with one in mind, she would always lead up to it by a reference to her superior's dress or a compliment about a change of policy one of them had made.

There was one thing that irritated Miss Quivey particularly. Patrons of the Library were not permitted to go into the upper stacks, and although this rule was known to most of them, from time to time some new patron or some stranger would stray unknowingly into that forbidden territory. Eventually some staff member would see the person wandering around up there and would hurriedly dispatch a page to inform him of the rule.

When Miss Quivey first observed this condition, she just couldn't help saying to herself what poor management it was, what a waste of effort! The last library she had worked in – things had been very different there! Patrons of that library had been permitted to go any place in the building that they wished. Miss Quivey heartily approved of such rules. But, she decided, so long as the policies of her new employers were somewhat narrower, she would just have to conform. When you were in Rome you had to do as the Romans did. But just the same, there was no sense whatsoever in wasting all that energy in chasing patrons out of the upper stacks. It was simply nonsense.

What they needed, Miss Quivey decided, was a sign. A neat little wooden sign, with gold letters on polished wood, like the ones at the desks that were marked Return, Loan, and Registration. She considered this idea for some time, and eventually she even hit upon the exact wording the proposed sign should have: The Upper Stacks are Closed to the Public. It was clear and curt. She thought of other signs, too. Patrons are not Allowed in the Upper Stacks was one of them, and she also pondered over For Staff Members Only, rejecting this as too harsh. Keep Out, Please came to her also, but she quickly disregarded it as a possibility of no consequence.

There was only one entrance to the upper stacks, and Miss Quivey discovered, when she examined the doorway, an ideal place for the sign to hang. It could be seen easily, and yet it would not hang so low that people might bump their heads on it. All in all, Miss Quivey was quite pleased with the place she had found for the sign to hang.

Then, several days later, when Miss Quivey was out at the charging desk with Miss Counselman, her department head, they both happened to notice a man in the upper stacks. He was just standing there, looking at the books on anatomy and sex.

"Oh, heavens!" Miss Counselman said. "Someone's up there in the uppers again. I'll have to send one of the boys up right this minute and get him out."

The circumstances could not have been better for Miss Quivey, and when Miss Counselman returned from telling one of the pages about the man in the stacks, she said, "Miss Counselman, why don't you have a sign made for the entrance over there?"

"What's that?" Miss Counselman asked.

"Why isn't there a sign over there telling people that they can't go into the uppers? It seems an awful waste of time and effort to have to keep watching out for people that go up there."

"Why, I never thought of that! That is a splendid suggestion, Miss Quivey. Now let's see, what should the sign say? Patrons Are Not Permitted to Use the Upper Stacks? No, that's too long. Let me see. The Upper Stacks Are For the Use of Staff Members Only? No, that's no good either. Now, let me think."

Miss Quivey smiled coolly. "What do you think of The Upper Stacks are Closed to the Public?"

"Excellent!" said Miss Counselman promptly. "Now let me write that down. Unless we can think of another better one, that's the one we'll use."

Just then someone came up to the desk and Miss Quivey could not continue her talk with Miss Counselman about the sign. She had wanted to talk about the composition of the sign, the gold letters on polished wood, and she had wanted to point out the ideal place from which it could be hung.

Miss Counselman left on her vacation several days later. From time to time Miss Quivey would think about their talk and wonder if Miss Counselman had made any arrangements about the sign before she left. Sometimes when she came down to work in the morning, she would go by the entrance to the upper stacks, hoping that the new sign would be hanging there. She knew, though, that it often took quite a while to get things done, and she tried to be patient.

But when Miss Counselman returned from her vacation and still nothing happened, it was most difficult for Miss Quivey to remain silent. Several times each day she tried to think of some manner in which she might bring the matter up without seeming to be over-anxious, and finally, as she passed Miss Counselman one morning in the open shelf room, she said, "Oh say, what about our little sign, Miss Counselman?"

"What sign is that?"

"The one for the uppers. You remember the day we were talking about it, don't you?"

"Well, for goodness sake!" Miss Counselman said. "I'm glad you reminded me of that, Miss Quivey. It had completely slipped my mind! I knew there was something I'd forgotten. Well, thank you for reminding me of it. That was such a splendid suggestion you made. Splendid, absolutely splendid!"

"Oh, that's all right, Miss Counselman," said Miss Quivey brightly.

But she was disappointed. A lot of time had passed already with nothing done, and there would be more delay, and all the while people would continue to wander into the stacks, and pages would have to be sent to remind them of the rule prohibiting their presence there. Miss Quivey began to feel somewhat hopeless about the whole business. And, too, it was only one of many, many things she saw that needed to be remedied. She consoled herself by thinking of the future, when she would be a head librarian or a department head. When that time came, things would be done right.

She kept looking for the sign, feeling that before long it would surely appear. Then one day when she was in the slipping room, months later, after she had almost forgotten about the sign, Miss Franks, a stylish young librarian whose morals were said to be not what they should, came in to talk to Miss Gates, who was working in the room with Miss Quivey. Miss Quivey had absolutely no use for Miss Franks.

Miss Franks had a sign in her hand. It was on polished wood, gold-lettered, and read: Patrons Are Not Allowed in the Upper Stacks.

Miss Franks ignored Miss Quivey altogether. "What do you think of the new sign, Opal?" she said to Miss Gates. She held it up in what Miss Quivey thought was a rather flippant manner, as if the sign were of no importance.

"Well now really!" Miss Gates said. "Now really, that's a very nice sign. And a mighty good idea, too. Who thought it up?"

"Oh, Miss Counselman, I guess," Miss Franks said. "You like it?"

"Why, it's just awfully nice!" Miss Gates said, taking a good look at it. "Let me see it! Well, that's about the best idea I've heard of in a long time. I don't know how many times I've said how badly we needed a sign like that."

"It's a nice little sign," Miss Franks said.

"It is!" said Miss Gates. "Where are you going to hang it?"

"I don't know," Miss Franks said without interest. "I'll find some place for it. Miss Counselman says she wants it put up right away."

It was too much. Miss Quivey had to stop slipping the cards for reserve books. She went to the staff room and stood by the couch for a long time, looking out of the window at the tulips that grew by the statue of ex-Mayor Spiegel. Cars kept going by the library and people walked along, and to Miss Quivey they seemed cruel and unheeding and unconcerned. No one knew, no one, how terribly she felt. There was no one to tell, there was no one to talk to, no one would sympathize. She was friendless and alone in the world, and she discovered that she was crying, and when she heard footsteps on the stairs she went into the dressing room and washed her face, wondering how she would ever get through the rest of the day.

It was terrible for her, and that night it was almost impossible for her to sleep. She lay awake on her studio couch, watching the pattern of automobile lights cutting across the ceiling, and listening to voices in the next apartment that came through the thin walls. She kept telling herself that she had to stop thinking about it.

Miss Quivey kept waiting for the day when she would come to work and see the sign hanging above the entrance to the upper stacks, even though it didn't seem to matter much any more. But something happened to the sign. She was never able to discover just what it was. She talked to Miss Gates and Miss Franks, but neither of them knew. Miss Franks had given it to one of the janitors to bore holes in it. Miss Quivey did not talk to any of the janitors. Miss Counselman got a much better job in another city about that time; and so there was no possibility of finding out from her where the sign was.

Patrons still wandered into the stacks by mistake, and staff members, seeing them up there, would summon a page to go up and tell them that the upper stacks were not open to the public. It made Miss Quivey furious every time she thought about it.

But she worried less about the sign than she had before. She was getting quite disturbed about some of the pages.

Some of them did not shave often enough. They came to work looking unkempt and their faces bristly with whiskers. One of them wore shirts that were not clean. She had observed several of them chewing gum. It didn't look good to see that sort of thing going on. She was going to speak to the staff member in charge of the pages about them, when she thought of the right approach. She didn't want anyone to think she was not keeping her place, though, or just going out of her way to be critical. She certainly didn't want them to feel that way.

FAREWELL TO FROGNALL

Sᴛ. Cʟᴀɪʀ had no intention of calling on Frognall, whom he did not know at all well and did not, as a matter of fact, like particularly; but he had become tired of walking about aimlessly and, finding himself in Frognall's neighborhood, decided to look in on him. The weather, too, had turned bitterly cold, and St. Clair had come out with only a thin topcoat. Frognall always prided himself on the warmth of his place.

Frognall had been living for some time now in a garage that had been converted into an apartment. To get to it entailed certain difficulties which St. Clair had almost forgotten. He was not even sure that the driveway into which he turned was the correct one. It was certainly equally as dark as the one that led to Frognall's. St. Clair crept along in the darkness, keeping one hand in front of him as a guard. There was no use in taking chances. The houses on each side of him were darkened. He lowered his hand momentarily and took a few more tentative steps. The last one was unfortunate, for he stepped into the spokes of a tricycle that a child had left in the driveway, and narrowly escaped falling flat on his face. He began to curse in a loud tone of voice, and, when he had recovered his balance, struck a match and took a look around. A huge and very vicious-appearing dog, suddenly awakened, began to bark furiously at St. Clair. He was terrified for a moment and then noted with relief that the animal and he were separated by a fence. He walked away with an air of outraged dignity, while the dog threw himself against the fence, still barking savagely.

St. Clair reflected that it must be the second driveway down. It was with a certain dim elation that he noted a light in Frognall's window. The wind was growing steadily colder. He rapped on the door and it was opened by Frognall.

St. Clair scarcely noticed Frognall at first, but looked beyond him to the front room. He was distressed to see it in such a state of disorder. Frognall had long been noted for a worship of neatness bordering, St. Clair felt, on the fanatical. But now the pictures had all been removed from the walls, exposing light squares and, in one instance, a very unsightly spot; there were piles of books and packing boxes everywhere; a disconnected radio trailed its wires like vines across the floor.

Frognall was blinking as though this aided him in attempting to recognize his visitor.

"Parsons?" he asked experimentally.

"It's St. Clair."

"Oh." Frognall's tone was skeptical. "Get in the light a bit more, will you?"

St. Clair obliged ill-naturedly.

"Oh, St. Clair," said Frognall. "I suppose you might as well come in."

When Frognall had closed and bolted the door, St. Clair looked about the room with an air of suspicion and disapproval, narrowing his eyes in the manner of a person enduring a dust-storm. The room was not at all as pleasant as he had remembered it. A mirror had been taken down and lay on its side against the wall, and he saw from the reflection it threw back that he badly needed a shine.

"There seems to be no place to sit," he observed.

Frognall said, "I'm moving."

"Yes?"

"Tomorrow. I have to be out of here by tomorrow. As long as you're here, you can help me pack."

"I'd like to," St. Clair said, without any particular eagerness. He stood by the door to the kitchen, looking at a sink full of rusty spoons and greasy dishes. A line of very large ants were crawling up the wall, where they disappeared behind a piece of pink-and-mauve oilcloth.

"I have all these books to be packed," Frognall said.

"There must be several thousand."

"About."

From one of the chairs St. Clair removed a drawing-board, a number of broken graham crackers, and what appeared to be a sort of harness, and, after taking off his topcoat, sat down and lit a cigarette.

"What have you been doing?" said Frognall. He was a tall man, no longer so very young, with bushy carrot-colored hair and bad teeth. He did not look straight at one when speaking.

St. Clair said, "Translating the poems of Gröbman-Pauli."

"Never heard of him."

"Few have. He is quite unknown here. His poems are virtually untranslatable and depend for their effectiveness on an almost unbearably tedious repetition of gutteral sounds. It is very difficult to reproduce their flavor in a translation. He wrote exclusively in septenaries. Little is known of his life. He abandoned poetry in his twenty-fourth year and seems to have allowed himself to be supported by women of a low sort from that point on until his death, a peculiarly revolting one at the age of forty."

"Who wrote, 'I come from haunts of coot and hern'?" Frognall asked.

"I haven't the faintest idea," St. Clair said. "I'm certain it wasn't Gröbman-Pauli."

"That line happened to occur to me."

St. Clair and Frognall were looking at each other. There seemed to be a sort of tension in the atmosphere. Just then the telephone rang. It was buried under a pile of soiled shirts and toilet articles on the floor, and it rang ten or twelve times before Frognall was able to extricate it. "Hello," he said. "Oh, it's you Vera. No. No. No, positively no. I'll call you tomorrow morning. No, there's no one here. If you call back I shan't answer. Goodnight, Vera."

St. Clair sat with a smug look while listening to this conversation.

"Do you want a drink?" Frognall asked. He was perspiring a good deal.

St. Clair brightened. This was more than he had counted on. Frognall had rarely been known to offer anyone a drink, except to girls he brought to his place occasionally in the hopes of seducing them.

They went into the kitchen, from which St. Clair soon withdrew to stand in the doorway, since it was, he discovered, far too small to accommodate both of them in comfort. Frognall was taking bottles down from a cabinet and, in some cases, holding them up to the light.

"A finger of rum," he said. "An inch or two of gin. This was given to me by that ski expert who was in town a few months ago posing as a British lord. He took everyone in." Frognall put the bottle down on a shelf by the sink. "Rye. Fully a quarter of a pint there. Scotch. Scarcely enough to cover the bottom of the bottle. More rye. More gin. I don't know why I've been hanging on to this empty cognac bottle."

By the time he had finished, there were fully a dozen bottles, each of them nearly empty, but collectively representing a decent amount of liquor.

"Ah, here's another," Frognall said. "A quart of brandy, and it's never been opened. Want to buy it?"

"What brand?"

"Uh, 'Old Badger' it seems to be called."

"Never heard of it."

"The man said it was very good."

"What did you pay for it?"

"Three and a half."

"Let me see it," St. Clair said.

Frognall handed it to him. The label was very beautifully printed but the lettering on it was rather difficult to read. Then St. Clair noticed something else. "It says here," he said sternly, "$1.89."

Frognall frowned. "Where does it say that?"

"Right here, in pencil."

"So it does. Strange. Oh, it must have been that it *was* three and a half, and then marked down to the other price."

"I don't think it can be very good brandy, Frognall. 'Old Badger.' Thank you, no."

"I'll let you have it for a dollar."

St. Clair debated the wisdom of the purchase. One could always serve it to people one did not want coming around again, he reflected. That could be done if it turned out to be as unpalatable as he somehow felt it would be. He gave Frognall a dollar.

"It's a pity I shan't be able to drink it," Frognall said, after having scrutinized the bill and put it in his pocket.

"Going on the wagon?"

"I'm leaving. For good."

"Oh?"

"The Army."

"Just hand me that bottle with the rye in it," St. Clair said. He took a long drink. "I thought you were a conscientious objector."

"I was. I was. But I've been doing some reading lately that has given me an entirely different slant on things," Frognall said. He poured out some gin in a glass and held it under the faucet, but no water came out when he turned it on. "I had them turn the water off today," he said rather wearily.

"We can drink it straight," St. Clair said. "You were saying?"

"Oh, yes. Some of the reading I've been doing lately has made me realize not only the folly of holding minority opinions in wartime, but the very real objections to the pacifist doctrine."

"I see."

"Then, too, I've not been much pleased to hear about the way conscientious objectors have been treated. And there's a chance, if things work out the way I hope they will, that I may fall into a very soft spot in the Army."

"I see," said St. Clair. He carried the bottle into the other room and sat down and drank some more rye.

"Can't you say something else but 'I see'?" Frognall asked.

"Not at the moment."

"I hope you're not planning on getting drunk," Frognall said. There was a peevish quality of reproach in his tone that irritated St. Clair. "I need help in packing these books."

"What do you want me to do?"

"A friend of mine is going to store them for me. Now, I want to know in which box each book will be, in case I should want to write for something. You pack the books and read me the title and author and I'll write it down. Then we can assign numbers to each box and put the same number on each sheet of paper."

"It seems like a lot of work, Frognall."

"Do you intend to help me or don't you?"

"Very well."

"I'll have to ask you to stop drinking my liquor if you're not going to help."

"Any particular place you want to start?"

Frognall brought out a large packing box. "We'll begin," he

said, "with this pile," indicating one nearby. He watched St. Clair, who still hung on to the bottle, as he got down on the floor. Satisfied that he was about to repay him for the liquor he had not known how to dispose of anyway, Frognall picked up a pad of paper with a red cover and a picture of an Indian Chief on it and said, "Are you ready?"

"I suppose so." St. Clair opened the book on top of the pile. "*Tumors of Domestic Animals*, by Heriani Forepaugh," he read.

Frognall wrote and St. Clair put the book in the box. "Next."

"*An Introduction to Missionary Service*, by Georgina Anne Gollock."

"Next."

"*Gazophylacium Divinae Dilectionis*. No author."

"No author?"

"Not on the title page."

"Go on. What's the next one?"

"*Strange Holiness*, by Robert P. Tristram Coffin."

"Next."

"*Simple Conjuring Tricks Anyone Can Do*, by Wlademirus Goldwag," said St. Clair. "This is certainly an eerie little collection you have here, Frognall."

"These books represent fifteen years of collecting," Frognall said coldly.

St. Clair picked up several books. "*Meet Mr. Coyote*, by A.V. Meelbom," he said. "*Down Woodbrook Ways: Poems*, by Hannah Horgan Burrell. 'How to Punch the Bag,' by W.H. Rothwell."

"Not so fast."

St. Clair finished the bottle. He felt the liquor burning a hole the size of a silver dollar in the pit of his stomach. He sat looking questioningly at a red rubber glove lying on the windowsill. It impressed him. It gave him a momentary sense of loss and emptiness. How symbolic it was! he thought.

He picked up the next book, aware that Frognall had finished writing. "*Where Knowledge Means Happiness: A Handbook of Facts and Practical Procedure for Conserving Throughout Married Life the Rapture of Honeymoon Days,* " he said. "The author is Vee Perlman."

"Just the brief title, St. Clair. Next."

"*A Study of Dance Halls in Pittsburgh, Made Under the Auspices of the Pittsburgh Girls' Conference,* 1925, by Collis A. Stocking."

"The *brief* title only, St. Clair," said Frognall, giving him a reproachful look.

The telephone made a strange brittle noise. It was the operator telling Frognall to put the receiver back on the hook.

"What in God's name induces you to buy such books as these?" St. Clair said, when Frognall had completed his dealings with the operator.

"What's the matter with them?"

"I should hesitate to say. Have you read any of them?"

"I read '*How to Punch the Bag.*'"

St. Clair sighed. "Are you sure you don't have any water, Frognall?"

"I told you I had it turned off."

"I suppose I may as well finish up that other bottle of rye."

Frognall got it for him. As he was coming out of the kitchen, the telephone rang again. He handed the bottle to St. Clair and answered it. It was another girl, someone named Eloise. She seemed to be of a more insistent nature than Vera, for it took Frognall much longer to get rid of her. He seemed very distraught when he was finally able to hang up.

St. Clair was pretending to read a book called *Directions for Using the Patent Eagle Tanning Process* while listening to the conversation.

"These women!" Frognall said. "It's enough to drive you insane. I may as well tell you, St. Clair, that I've become horribly involved with two girls here in town. Horribly involved. You wouldn't dream. I've been living for weeks in absolute torment, and I finally decided that the only way out was either suicide or the Army." He lit a cigarette and puffed nervously.

St. Clair made no comment. He had just then noticed a section on the wall, where a large bookcase had once stood. It was covered with one of the most dreadful murals he had ever seen.

Frognall became aware of St. Clair's focus of interest. "Another girl did *that*," he said. "I just went out one night to go downtown – I couldn't have been gone more than an hour or so – and when I got back she had painted *that* on the wall."

"You in the Army," St. Clair said. "I can't get over it."

"You'll be there soon," Frognall said.

"Yes, I suppose so."

"I wish I were dead," Frognall said. He slumped down in his chair and began pounding his forehead with his fist. "There'll never be an end to it, St. Clair, this horrible, horrible world."

"That's right."

"We're all washed up," Frognall said. "Listen, do you know anyone who is happy?"

"Quite a few people," said St. Clair. "That's what makes it all the worse."

"Why do you go on living? Do you ever think about suicide?"

"All the time, practically. Except when I'm translating someone like Gröbman-Pauli."

Frognall sat there staring at the mural. "When I was a kid I used to dream about becoming a great violinist. Well, they gave me music lessons and it was discovered that I had no sense of time. Do you know what a thing like that can do to a person?"

St. Clair could not think of any comment to make. He had no gift for rising to the occasion when matters took this sort of turn.

"I can't do anything more with all this stuff tonight," Frognall said. "I'll have to do it in the morning. Go away, St. Clair."

"Do you want me to help—"

"Go away, St. Clair, go away."

Frognall was still sitting there, staring at the floor, when St. Clair took his leave. St. Clair went down the driveway and walked home. The cold air cleared his head a little. It had begun to snow. He unlocked the door to his room and took the bottle of brandy to a table, where he opened it. It was even worse than he had expected. It would do, though, for the unwanted guests. But even they were getting fewer and fewer. Everyone was going off to the wars. St. Clair undressed and got into bed. A military band was playing loudly on the radio downstairs, and it was a long time before he could get to sleep.

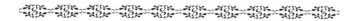

THE PURCELLS

THE HOUSE WAS LARGE, and white, with a vast veranda and surrounded by rose bushes; it had an ordered, almost severe air, and seemed only remotely related to the rooms that it enclosed. Viewed from a distance among the neighboring houses – red brick or gray stone, garnished with rusting iron-work – it gave the impression of one of those homes which paint companies are so fond of having photographed for reproduction in magazine advertisements. And I remember the shock I had felt when, as a child, I was first taken there, for the interior of the house gave a totally different impression.

I remember most vividly the brilliantly-colored totem pole that stood in the hall. It was the first thing one saw when the door was opened by the Purcells' maid. Mr. Purcell had brought the totem pole back from an Alaskan trip they had made and, finding it too large to stand upright in any of the rooms, had cut it in two. The largest section was given a commanding place in the hall, directly in front of the door, while the rest of it, looking strangely disembodied (Mr. Purcell had sawed through one of the faces) lingered nearby. But these objects were only a preparation for other surprises.

Behind the door was a wax figure of Martha Washington in a soiled blue dress (someone had left a burn in the front of it with a cigar), and close inspection revealed that its right eyelash had become unglued, hanging spiderishly by one corner. There was an umbrella-stand of hammered copper, with some sort of a crest on one side, bearing a motto in Latin; it was crammed with umbrellas and canes of an endless variety. In another corner was a stuffed lioness, with bared teeth and a stiff tongue of dirty pink, and a tail that swung when it was touched. The rug was straw; people were always tripping over it.

Yet the hall gave less of an impression of clutter and general disorder than did the living room, which, it was said, had cost more to complete than any room in town. The room could have been quite handsome, with its dark walls of paneled wood and its leaded windowpanes, its great chandelier and oriental rugs; but these were obscured by the scratched (and untuned) grand piano, covered by a vast batik cloth of appalling hideousness, and in turn littered by stacks of books (unread, and still in their dust-jackets), best-sellers of a few years back; dog-eared sheet music; piles of Christmas cards; a glass ball that, when agitated, surrounded the little castle which it enclosed with languid flurries of snow; bills and letters and purses; vases filled with half-withered flowers and dried berries, some of which had fallen off; plates of candy and cookies, which had been there for a long time and had become hard and inedible; rubber balls and other objects for the amusement of Mrs. Purcell's current dog. (There were seven or eight of these through the years, all Boston bulldogs, all female, all quite stupid, and all named 'Betsy Bobbitt,' and all alike, so far as I could tell, except for one which had had something wrong with one of its eyes.) At the windows were green curtains of a heavy corded silk; these were drawn together most of the time. The house smelled of incense and candles and of Mr. Purcell's cigars; there were always cigar-ends lying about. Most astonishing were the many chimes, or whatever it is that they are called

– those arrangements of glass rectangles like laboratory slides, which dangle from pieces of string and are usually found on porches, where they tinkle feebly in the wind. Mrs. Purcell had the house filled with these devices, and it will give some indication of the draughty nature of the house to set down the fact that they were seldom quiet. There must have been thirty or forty clocks; most of them had run down and had never been wound again, and the others were hours off. They were constantly striking, and no one paid any attention to them; I doubt if Mrs. Purcell was conscious of time at all.

That first day, when I was taken there by my aunt, I was presented to Mrs. Purcell, who kissed me wetly, said I was a lovely little boy, and gave me a piece of stale candy from a plate on the piano. She smelled of face powder and I decided that I didn't like her. She was very buxom and was wearing a dark dress with a heavy beaded collar that looked as if the dressmaker had not yet completed work on it. (I was to learn later that, although Mrs. Purcell thought nothing of spending two or three hundred dollars on an imported shawl, which she might never again look at after acquiring it, she prided herself on the fact that most of her dresses were picked up at sales for $13.95.)

My aunt told me, as she and Mrs. Purcell sat down, that I should play with the dog, which was curled up on a hooked rug before the fireplace. I understood that they did not wish me lurking about as they talked, and I approached the dog, who opened one eye as I knelt down by it, sniffed at me, and returned to its nap. I had not liked the look of the piece of candy which had been given me and still held it in the moist palm of my hand, where it had begun to get unpleasantly sticky. I looked around for a place to dispose of it and dropped it in a large Chinese vase, which rang like a gong; turning, I was relieved to discover that Mrs. Purcell and my aunt were too engrossed in what they were saying to each other to be aware of what I had done. I sat down on the floor and began to look through some old copies of the *Mentor*, which were piled between a luxuriant fern and a rounded glass inclosure containing a number of stuffed birds.

"The genealogist I have working for me in Washington has discovered *another* revolutionary ancestor of mine," Mrs. Purcell was saying to my aunt in a pleased tone. "Isn't that lovely?"

"Oh, how lovely for you, Grace," said my aunt, who was almost as interested in other persons' families as in her own.

Mrs. Purcell then went on to give an account of the prolonged and untiring researches of her genealogist in the East, who had unearthed the 'new' Revolutionary War ancestor from a hitherto-undiscovered branch of Mrs. Purcell's family, a branch which, it appeared, opened up whole new vistas of investigation.

Mrs. Purcell had moved on to an account of the last meeting of the D.A.R., which my aunt had been prevented from attending because of a cold, when I heard a door open on the second floor and the sound of rapid footsteps on the stair. Mr. Purcell burst into the room, waving a sheet of paper. He was a tall, thin man with a sharp nose and cold gray eyes. "Grace, what in God's name have you done to this thing?" he exclaimed. It was not until he had got this out that he noticed that his wife had visitors. Even then he appeared anything but embarrassed, and only grinned in a way that seemed to invite us to share his irritation for something absurd that his wife had done. He explained to my aunt, as an old friend, the nature of Mrs. Purcell's error in filling out some kind of a blank he had given her. He had an explosive manner of speech; and, as he sat down, I had the feeling that he lived in a permanent state of tension, while his wife,

somehow bovine and not very intelligent, enjoyed an existence of subnormal calm, which his outbursts ruffled only
faintly.

He had begun to talk of a new rose bush with which he
had been experimenting and grew quite excited about it,
when my aunt asked him about his friend, Charles Oakes,
who had recently been elected Governor of the State and
whom everyone expected would appoint Mr. Purcell to
some important State office. But the maid came in at that
moment to inform Mr. Purcell that someone was waiting to
see him, and, after he had excused himself, my aunt looked
at her watch, exclaimed at the lateness of the hour and said
that we, too, must go.

After that I was taken many times to the Purcells' and we
saw them frequently elsewhere. It was from my aunt that I
learned that Ernest Purcell had come from a poor middle-
western family and had grown up on a farm. He had worked
his way through an agricultural college, where he had stayed
on as a graduate student, writing a Master's thesis on some
obscure aspect of crop rotation. After teaching for a few
years, he had been hired by D. G. Akers, a wealthy farmer,
who owned several counties of extremely fertile farm land,
as a sort of overseer and manager. Shortly after that he had
married Grace Akers, his employer's only child.

They had been married only a few months when his wife
had begun to suffer from some mysterious glandular disorder, by which medical specialists confessed themselves
baffled. She had been a very pretty and slender girl at the
time of their marriage, it was said, but within six months she
looked twice her age and had grown puffy and swollen. Her
weight had increased seventy or eighty pounds. I saw a
photograph of them taken before they left on their honeymoon; he was slim and handsome and she seemed very
attractive, too, and I had difficulty in connecting her with
the fat, eccentric woman who was my aunt's friend.

Her father died not long after this peculiar ailment began, and Grace Purcell inherited everything he owned, becoming thereby one of the wealthiest women in the entire middlewest. The summer following her father's death, she and her husband had gone on a world cruise, during the course of which they visited several European specialists who they hoped might be able to throw some light on the nature of Mrs. Purcell's state of health and do something about it. Various attempts were made, but none of them had any effect.

From that time on they traveled a good deal, mainly, I gathered, at her insistence. Mr. Purcell himself was never happier than when visiting his wife's farms, conferring with the tenants and making suggestions to them in an excited tone of voice. I think he was deeply disappointed when his friend, Charles Oakes, offered him only a minor political office which he declined, considering it beneath him. He and Mrs. Purcell went to California for a long stay, and for once, I believe, he was glad to go.

Mrs. Purcell had various interests – in staying at large and expensive hotels, in the knowledge that several of her ancestors had taken part in the Revolutionary War, in certain smallscale charities, and particularly in the pleasure of buying, which she gratified almost incessantly. She liked nothing better than to spend whole days in department stores, accumulating anything that caught her bizarre and undiscriminating fancy. She was particularly given to a mania for shawls and bedspreads, and at the time of her death she had over three hundred shawls and almost as many bedspreads, many of which had never been unwrapped since she had bought them. It was her usual practice to come home with the back seat of the car filled with packages, which the chauffeur would carry into Mrs. Purcell's bedroom, where they might remain for days before she would have the maid put them in one of the many guest rooms. Two of these were so crammed with unwrapped packages that they had come to be regarded as storerooms and were never heated. The craze for bedspreads and shawls remained constant throughout her life; there were others that lasted anywhere from a month to a year – for Japanese prints, andirons, china dolls, beaded bags, Victrola records, jewelry, clocks, Oriental rugs.

Mr. Purcell was never able to become accustomed, let alone resigned, to his wife's buying orgies, and during the Depression he frequently complained to anyone who would listen that they were headed straight for the poorhouse. I think he enjoyed nothing more than painting a dark picture of a poverty-striken end for both of them; but Mrs. Purcell was quite unmoved by her husband's forebodings. She knew very well that she could afford to be quite as extravagant as she wished.

As they grew older, they both found difficulty in remaining awake. The Purcells sat in front of us in church. Not long after the sermon had begun, their heads would nod and they would soon fall into a prolonged but, fortunately, quiet slumber. On the occasion, Mr. Purcell, who was in the habit of putting his fingers into the holes used for holding communion glasses, neglected to take them out before falling asleep; when he was awakened by a blast from the organ and the shrill voices of the choir, he discovered that his fingers had become so swollen that he could not remove them. I believe it was necessary, finally, to send for a carpenter before Mr. Purcell was able to leave the church.

They also slept in theatres. Several times my aunt and I went with them, and they always dozed, but never would either of them admit that they had been anything else than wide awake. Coming out of the theatre, both would comment on how enjoyable the picture had been. They were quick to change the subject, however, if a detailed discussion of the film arose.

Yet in spite of their few eccentricities, they led lives of the utmost respectability – large contributors to the church, to civic and patriotic and charitable organizations, voting the straight Republican ticket, and, I think, well satisfied, on the whole, with their existences.

When moving-picture cameras for home use became popular, Mr. Purcell took to this branch of photography with a zest that he had formerly displayed only for agriculture and for Henry Ford. (I ought to mention here that Mr. Purcell carried the frequently-encountered worship of the Detroit manufacturer further than I have ever observed it carried by anyone else. He had a large scrapbook filled with clippings about Ford, and the only book I ever heard him refer to – except for something of Sinclair Lewis's, which he described to me as 'indescribable filth' and tried to get the Public Library to burn – successfully, as I recall – was Ford's *My Life and Work*, which he had had bound in heavy tooled leather and which he re-read constantly, wearing an expression of deep contentment.) His moving-picture camera accompanied the Purcells on their trips, and Mr. Purcell would always return with several large reels, documenting, practically, their every move. He would exhibit these to their friends in the darkened living room after dinner, his voice high and nasal above the whirr of the projector: "That's Grace at Annapolis, talking to Roscoe VanOrsdale, who is a cadet there and a mighty fine young man. This is a picture of the cadets on parade; it's not very clear because the light wasn't very good that day, and it's sort of jerky right here because Betsy Bobbitt had got hold of my trouser-leg and I was trying to shake her off while I was taking the picture.... This is one of Grace's cousins in her garden in Philadelphia; that arm you see on the right side of the screen, waving a water lily, belongs to a friend of hers; now she's coming into the picture. She's a very good friend of Mrs. Dwight Morrow...."

That's Betsy Bobbitt on the steps of Independence Hall; we'd given her some salt-water taffy – that's what's making her chew that way."

Mrs. Purcell seemed to find it less difficult to remain awake at her husband's movies than at others, perhaps, it was said, because of the interest she took in her own film personality. But she was not always able to keep her eyes open, and it was at about this time that her period of silent sleep gave way to a sleep characterized by restlessness and snoring. There was one appalling evening when, just as a view of some of Mr. Purcell's prize hogs, wallowing and grunting in a muddy pen, was thrown on the screen for us to admire, Mrs. Purcell, who had fallen asleep a few moments before, began to snore in a ghastly animal fashion. Someone snickered. It was a horrible moment, and for a while one scarcely dared to breathe. When, at length, the lights were turned on, Mrs. Purcell awakened and smiled brightly at her guests as though she had been awake all the time.

It was only a few months after this that her health began to fail and she was forced to spend more and more of her time in bed. She was a fretful and unruly patient: with her buying expeditions, travels and genealogical forays cut down, she had little to fall back on for amusement. She was unable to keep her mind on anything to read for more than ten to fifteen minutes, and she was not sufficiently patient to sew. And the delicacies she most enjoyed – rich puddings and pies and cakes – were now denied her. Yet she grew fatter and fatter; her eyes, encased in heavy folds of skin, seemed to sink more deeply into her face. She was allowed to get up and dress now and then, but her clothes were much too small for her, though she refused to recognize this fact and would not have them altered. – After a while she was not permitted to leave her bed; it was said she was dying.

In the meantime, news of the shame of Mr. Purcell's

middle age was spreading, and was late, I think, in reaching us. He had become wildly infatuated with a young woman who worked at the soda fountain of one of the downtown drugstores, and spent most of his time there, eating a great deal of ice cream and talking to her. Her name was Leona Higgins. She had previously been a chicken-picker at a meat-packing plant, and had a husband, a sometime barber who played drums occasionally with a local five-piece danceband. When my aunt learned that Mr. Purcell was seeing this woman constantly, she was outraged and disturbed; she saw Mrs. Purcell almost daily and felt sure that sooner or later she was bound to learn of her husbands monstrous fall from grace.

Mr. Purcell no longer attended church and paid less and less attention to his work. He visited his tenants infrequently and was given to flying into inexplicable fits of temper. He was almost certain to be found at the drugstore or at the apartment of the Higginses, who lived over a second-hand furniture store not far from the railroad tracks. He and Higgins seemed on the best of terms, and the three of them were often to be observed driving around town in Mr. Purcell's Cadillac. They spent many evenings sitting in the Higgins' kitchen, matching nickles and drinking beer. When Higgins had a dance job in some nearby town, Mr. Purcell would drive the three of them over; sometimes he and Mrs. Higgins would dance, but usually they sat out in the Cadillac, listening to the music.

I have never learned who it was that informed Mrs. Purcell; some said that an anonymous letter was delivered to her. However she did get the news, she went into a blind rage and neither her maid nor her nurse were able to prevent her from getting out of bed and dressing. She was huge: she put on an old white lace dress of hers that split up the sides as she got into it, and when the nurse tried to keep her from leaving, Mrs. Purcell struck her with her arm and rushed from the house. She must have been headed for the drugstore: she was within a block of it when she fell dead in the street, in front of a poolhall.

It was a magnificent funeral, although the burial itself was marred by a heavy rainstorm. Mr. Purcell came with the Higginses. A great many of the Purcell's former friends refused to speak to him. When we drove away in the rain back to town, I saw him standing by the grave, talking to Higgins, a wiry little man with a beaked nose.

He inherited everything of hers, of course. The Higginses moved into the big house with Mr. Purcell; and, going by there, one might often hear Higgins playing "Chopsticks" or "Twelfth Street Rag" on the piano.

It was a month or so after Mrs. Purcell died that I paid my last visit to their home. My aunt had found, in her bookcase, a book which she had borrowed some time before from Mrs. Purcell; when she discovered Mr. Purcell's name written on the flyleaf, she declared that she would not have it in the house and I offered to return it. "Just leave it in the mailbox," my aunt said, but I had no intention of doing so, for I was curious to discover in what manner the life in that house had changed. The town was full of stories of Mr. Purcell; of his reckless driving, his bloodshot eyes, and his unpredictable changes in temper – one moment he would be talking to you quite soberly and then suddenly would go off into a fit of laughter or blind rage. – As I walked up the hill and turned down the long, tree-shaded street, I felt excited and a bit apprehensive about my errand.

There was still a black wreath on the door, and, as I stood ringing the bell, the last of the dogs known as Betsy Bobbitt raced around the corner of the veranda, her jaws fastened on an open newspaper, over which she tripped repeatedly as she went past me and disappeared around the other side of the house.

The door was suddenly flung open, after I had rung a second time, revealing Mrs. Higgins. She was wearing a fantastic Spanish costume with spangles on it; she was violently made up and from her ears long black earrings dangled. I realized that her dress was surely one of those that Mr. Purcell had brought back from one of their world tours; and I could see that it had been amateurishly altered.

"Is Mr. Purcell here?" I asked.

"Yeh, Ernie's here," she said, running her tongue across her teeth and looking at me appraisingly.

"I wonder if I might see him for a minute."

"Why not? Come on in."

There were no noticeable changes in the hall, but in the living room I saw the piano for the first time denuded of its coverings. The batik cloth and the rest of the objects making up that wild collection were gone; there was only the bare, scratched top of the piano, decorated by an empty beer bottle and an ashtray.

Mr. Purcell was stretched out in a chair, smoking a cigar and engaged in conversation with Higgins. Both were in their shirt-sleeves and neither had shaved for several days. Higgins was eating something unpleasant-looking from a bowl.

"Well, hello there," Mr. Purcell said, looking up as I came into the room. He sounded a bit cool. "You haven't been around for quite a little while."

I said that I was returning a book that belonged to him, and laid it on a table.

"You know Bill Higgins here, I guess," Mr. Purcell said.

I had met him once and I greeted him.

"And that," Mr. Purcell said, "that right behind you is our little Spanish girl, Mrs. Higgins. Leona. Yesterday she was a little Dutch girl, wasn't she Bill? Huh?"

"That's a fact, Ernie," Higgins agreed, taking the spoon from his mouth. I noticed that Higgins' drums were set up near the piano. The head of the bass drum was ornamented by an oil painting of a moonlight lake scene.

"And the day before ... I've forgotten what she was the day before," Mr. Purcell said.

"That was the day we got so drunk and you run us in the ditch," Mrs. Higgins said.

Mr. Purcell began to laugh. I had never seen him so amused. Then the smile faded from his face and I became aware that he was looking fixedly at me. "Yes, and you can stop spreading those dirty stories about me and that girl out on the farm," he said to me.

I felt Mrs. Higgins tugging at my sleeve.

"Don't pretend you don't know what I'm talking about!" Mr. Purcell said. "Don't kid me, you dirty little sneak."

Even as he said this, I saw that his attention was wandering, that he had been distracted. He was looking at something beyond me. I turned and saw the dog called Betsy Bobbitt standing in the doorway. In her mouth was a dirty rubber ball.

"Who let that goddamn dog in here?" Mr. Purcell demanded. He looked around the room and, when no one replied, said angrily to the dog, "Come here. Come here, you."

The dog moved forward warily. So suddenly that I caught my breath, Mr. Purcell lunged at it, grabbed it by its collar and began beating it with his fist in a cold fury. Veins stuck out on his forehead. The first blow must have knocked the wind out of the dog, because it made no sound at all.

I was angry and disgusted and I turned and left the house, fully expecting someone to stop me. Just as I reached the porch steps I heard a cry from the dog and then Mr. Purcell came to the door and shouted something at me that I could not understand. He slammed the door behind him so hard that the windows rattled. As I went down the walk I heard Higgins playing "Shine, Little Glowworm" on the piano with one finger.

That was the last I saw of any of them. Shortly afterwards they went to California to live. Mr. Purcell hired another man to look after his farms. They live in a suburb of Los Angeles and spend a lot of time at the horseraces. Mr. Purcell has dyed his hair black, and it is said that he made the Higginses his sole heirs.

THREE YOUNG PRIESTS

THE THREE YOUNG PRIESTS came out of the drugstore after buying cigars. It was a chilly grey day, damp and unpleasant.

—I almost forgot, the tall priest said. He stood on the corner, frowning and scratching his chin.

—What's that? The fat one asked.

—Gloves, the tall priest said. I wanted to get some gloves.

—What kind? The fat one asked. He watched a girl in a brown coat going by.

—Oh, gloves, the tall priest said vaguely, glancing at the girl himself. Look at there. He held out his hands. They're all worn out, he said.

The fat priest and the one with the mole on his nose looked gravely at the tall priest's worn black gloves. They nodded their heads.

—Yes, you need some new ones, the fat priest said. You certainly need some new ones.

—I've been putting it off for a long time, the tall priest said.

—Those are very worn, said the fat priest.

The priest with the mole on his nose said nothing. He stuck his bare hands in his overcoat pockets and looked curiously at a sign in the drugstore window. It advertised a new kind of razor blade.

—Let's go down to that department store on the corner, the tall priest said. What's the name of it?

—The Famous.

—The Famous, the tall priest said. That's right.

They walked down the street. The three of them walking abreast on the sidewalk took up a good deal of room. People looked at them with interest as they passed, but the three young priests seemed to be unaware of them. The one with the mole on his nose looked in the store windows while the other two talked of Father Moran's appendicitis operation. The priest with the mole on his nose seemed to take no interest at all in the discussion. When they came to the department store he held the door open for them and followed them inside.

It was quite warm in the store. All the clerks were busy with customers, and the young priests stood quietly by one of the counters, looking at the signs announcing the January sale.

—They do a fine business, the fat priest observed.

—Um, the tall priest said.

—You may be able to get gloves cheaper than ordinarily.

—What's that?

—The sale they're having now.

—Oh yes, the sale, the tall priest said. Yes, that may make a difference.

The priest with the mole on his nose fingered some striped neckties on the counter. They were marked 98c. The fat priest looked about the store with interest. After a while the tall priest began to drum on the glass top of the counter with his fingers.

—Poor service, he said.

—Very, said the fat priest.

—But then, the tall priest said hurriedly, they're very busy.

—They are; they certainly are. The fat priest was beginning to perspire, and unbuttoned his overcoat. Hot in here, he remarked.

The priest with the mole on his nose walked over to another counter and looked at some initialed handkerchiefs which had been marked down from 50c to 29c. Then he discovered a three-way mirror. He stood in front of it, examining his profile.

Finally a young man wearing a grey suit hurried up to them. He smiled and said,—is anyone helping you yet?

—Not as yet, the tall priest said somewhat testily. I'd like to get some gloves.

—Gloves, the young man said. Hmm. Now let me see. Just what did you have in mind? Something like the ones you're wearing?

—Well, I don't know whether I want ones like these again or not. They wore out in a hurry. Didn't last at all.

—I have something very nice here in a grey suede glove, the young man said, turning around and taking a pair from a drawer behind him. These are very nice, he said. He put them down on the counter in front of the tall priest.

The tall priest looked at them for a moment and then shook his head. —No, he said, I don't think I want anything like that.

—It's a nice number, the young man said.

—I'm afraid not for me.

—Well, how about something in a calfskin, perhaps? the young man asked.

—Yes, maybe. Perhaps something like these I have on. Only I'd like to have something that would stand wear better then these.

—Yes, sir, the young man said. He took a black pair from another drawer. These should be about your size. Why don't you try them on, just for fit.

The tall priest took off the old gloves and tried on the right one of the new pair. It was slightly stiff, but he had only a little difficulty in getting it on.

—Those are nice, the fat priest observed.

—What are the price of these? the tall priest asked. He paid no attention to the fat priest.

—Three dollars, the young man said. With the sale discount, two seventy.

—Those are nice gloves, the fat priest said.

The tall priest was feeling of the surface of the glove of his left hand. Suddenly he turned around and looked about the store.

—Where did Tim go? He said.

The fat priest turned and looked also.

—Why, he was here just a minute ago. I thought he was right here with us.

—Well, that's strange where he went.

—No, he was here just a minute ago.

—He couldn't have gone far.

—Funny.

—He was right over by those handkerchiefs.

—Oh, there he is, the fat priest said.

—Where?

—There. See? Back there by those dressing gowns.

—Oh, so he is. The tall priest turned back to the clerk. What did you say the price of these is?

—Two seventy during the sale, the clerk said. Marked down from three dollars.

—Let me try on the other glove.

—Oh, certainly, the clerk said, handing it to him.

—Those are mighty nice gloves, the fat priest said admiringly. I'll have to get some myself before long.

The tall priest took quite a little time stretching his hands in the new gloves.

—That's an excellent fit, the clerk said. They may feel a little stiff just now, but once your hands get worked into them, I'm sure they'll be just right. It's a mighty nice glove.

—I like them very much, the fat priest said.

The tall priest stretched his fingers in the new gloves, looking down at them suspiciously. —Two seventy, you said? he asked.

—Yes, sir, the clerk said. Two seventy. Marked down from three dollars during our January sale.

—They look like good quality, the fat priest said.

—They're very fine gloves, the clerk said, shifting his weight from one leg to another.

The tall priest held his fingers out straight and looked for a long time at the new pair of gloves. —Well, he said finally, I guess I'll take them. I guess I might just as well take them.

—Yes, sir, the clerk said, taking his salesbook from his pocket and looking at some customers that were waiting. Charge?

—No, I'll pay for them.

The fat priest felt of the new gloves on the tall priest's hands. —You've got a nice pair of gloves there, he said quietly.

The clerk finished making out his sales slip and looked up expectantly. —That'll be two seventy, he said.

The tall priest frowned. —What about the discount to the clergy? he asked. What about that?

The clerk looked at him perplexedly. —The discount to the clergy?

—Yes, yes, the tall priest said impatiently. The ten percent discount to the clergy.

—Just a minute, sir, the clerk said. He turned and walked down the narrow aisle back of the counter and talked for a while to a white-haired man who kept nodding his head. The tall priest frowned and drummed on the counter with his fingers. Finally the clerk returned and said, Sorry, I didn't know about that. Sorry. He figured rapidly on his sales slip. That'll be two forty-three, he said, looking up.

—Two forty-three, the tall priest said. I'd think it would be two forty, even.

—No, sir, I'm sorry, two forty-three is correct. Ten percent of two seventy is twenty seven cents less two seventy leaves two forty-three. The clerk showed the tall priest his figures.

The tall priest looked up from the numbers, scowling slightly, and said, —Oh, very well, very well. He took out his billfold and counted out the exact change.

—Do you want to wear the new gloves? the clerk asked. I'll put the old ones in a sack for you.

The tall priest merely nodded. The clerk took the old gloves and put them in a sack and twisted the end of it and handed it to the tall priest. —Thank you very much, he said.

Just then the priest with the mole on his nose came up.

—Where were you, Tim? the tall priest asked.

The priest with the mole nodded towards the back part of the store.

—Just back there, he said.

—Looking at ladies' underwear, eh? the fat priest asked jovially.

The tall priest cleared his throat and glared at both of them.

They walked out of the store. The priest with the mole on his nose held the door open for the other two. Already it was much darker on the street. They stood in front of the store for a moment, not saying anything.

Finally the tall priest said, —Well, where did we leave the car? Then he noticed that the priest with the mole on his nose was looking at him penetratingly. Well, what's the matter, anyway?

—Your bib's out, the priest with the mole said.

The tall priest looked down at himself quickly and tucked it inside his vest. Then he looked up and said again, —Now where did we leave the car? His face was quite red.

—I think we left it in front of that theatre by the postoffice, the fat priest said.

—So we did, the tall priest said, his face clearing. So we did.

—I'm pretty sure that's where we left it, the fat priest said.

—I know we did, said the tall priest. I'm positive of it.

The three young priests walked down the street, the mist gathering about them. The priest with the mole on his nose looked disinterestedly in the store windows, his hands in his overcoat pockets.

—You got a nice pair of gloves, the fat priest said. He took out a cigar and stripped the cellophane from it.

The tall priest merely nodded and glanced down at the new pair.

—Yes, a mighty nice pair of gloves, the fat priest went on. He bit off the end of his cigar.

They walked along the street and turned the corner in the direction of the theatre. It was very misty and rain was beginning to fall.

THE LIFE OF THE MIND

TOO MANY THINGS were weighing on Dr. Peate's mind. There was his wife, for one thing. He did not know whether she was dead or alive. He hoped she was dead. He had called his hotel at three o'clock, but there had been no word, no telegram or phone call from the hospital. He wished they would let him know. They really ought to let him know one way or another. Cerebral hemorrhage, they had said. It was a very dangerous business.

Then there was this matter of Jackson, the football player, who had called to say that he would be over in a few minutes. Dr. Peate looked out of his office window, across the campus. He saw Jackson, in a red sweater, hulking along past Jarvis Hall. There were so many of these issues that came up all the time for Dr. Peate to straighten out.

Dr. Peate held the Harry Gunnison White Chair of English Literature at the State University, and was in charge of the instructors who taught Freshman English (English 101–108). He had played tackle as an undergraduate, and still retained an abnormally active interest in football. For many years he had taken it upon himself to see that all football players got through their English courses without too much difficulty.

Dr. Peate lived by himself on the eleventh floor of the Whittier Hotel. He had been separated from his wife for some years. His whole married life had been unfortunate, and when he thought of it at all, he thought of it as "a tragic mistake." During the first year he had taught, he had foolishly and hastily married the best-looking girl in his classes. That had been at a girls' school in Missouri. She had been extravagant, silly, and too insatiable in a certain way for Dr. Peate, whose hiking activities seemed to take a lot out of him. At one time he had been first vice-president of a national hiking association. When he had come North to work on his Ph.D., his wife had bothered him incessantly when he was trying to write. She could not even type, and refused to learn; and he had had to spend a good deal of money getting his thesis typed by a woman who charged him exorbitantly. He had dedicated his thesis—on Nature in the writings of Charles Lamb—to the memory of his mother. His mother had been a stout woman with a fervent interest in women's rights and Navajo rugs.

Five years after he had married Gloria, she had run away with a man who operated a roach-exterminating concern in Chicago. Dr. Peate went to Chicago after her, very much perturbed, and found her alone in a disreputable hotel on Woodlawn Avenue. Her lover, the roach-exterminator, had abandoned her. Gloria had learned of two other wives that he had neglected to tell her about; perhaps there were others. Dr. Peate had been overjoyed to see his wife. Their reunion had been tender. They had been happier then than at any other time since their courtship and engagement. Dr. Peate took her to see Otis Skinner in *Kismet*, which was playing in Chicago at the time. He got $3.30 seats, the best in the house. The next day they returned to University City by train. She cried frequently and told him repeatedly how ashamed she was and that from then on she would be a good wife to him.

She wasn't. For several weeks she cooked, baked, cleaned, scrubbed, and mended his clothes, sewing the buttons on his shirts with so much thread that they were difficult to fasten into the buttonholes. After the several weeks, she gave up. The house became run-down and dirty. She began to go around with the wife of a man in the Sociology Department, a Pole, who got her started smoking and drinking. They went to many movies and sent away for photographs of Rudolph Valentino. Dr. Peate became terribly afraid for his reputation. He lectured to her a great deal, but it had no effect. Sometimes she laughed at him. She ridiculed his Sunday hikes. She refused to accompany him to football and basketball games, and put on a good deal of weight. She changed the manner of fixing her hair almost weekly, and when it began to turn gray, dyed it herself with something that caused her scalp to take on a strange green color.

She took up with fortune tellers. One night he had come back to a dinnerless home to find her sprawled out on the davenport, drunk, her hair falling every which way. There were playing cards scattered over the floor beside the davenport, and in her hand she had the ace of spades, which she waved at him frenziedly. "Death!" she said drunkenly. "Death! You're going to die, Jim Peate!"

He had her put away in the Woodlawn Hospital for Mental Cases. It cost him a good deal. Occasionally he went down to see her, but she no longer recognized him. She was perfectly happy and totally harmless so long as she had plenty of movie magazines to look at. She cut out the pictures and filled many scrapbooks with them.

It was shortly after he put his wife in the Woodlawn Hospital that Dr. Peate began to take an absorbing interest in the destinies of football players. He defended them at every chance, took them out to dinner, sometimes going along with them on out-of-town trips. He got a good deal of pity from people because of his broken home, especially from faculty wives. He was frequently asked out to dinner, and people never failed to mention how jovial and entertaining Dr. Peate could be, in spite of all the tragedy that had come into his life. They marveled at the knowledge he had of the world of sport, particularly at his ability to give the scores of any football game that was brought up. He liked their pity, too; but what he felt more than anything else when he went home at night was relief— relief that he did not have to face Gloria.

When Jackson arrived, Dr. Peate greeted him pleasantly and asked him to sit down while he attended to a little matter. He actually had nothing to attend to, but he often employed this technique when people came in. It showed he was a busy man.

He looked at his visitor, a two-hundred-pound young man wearing a red sweater. He needed a shave badly and was chewing on a match. He must be close to thirty, Dr. Peate thought. There was no use in dwelling on that, however. He could not help admiring Jackson's muscular arms and broad shoulders, recalling Jackson's admirable interference in Saturday's game. Jackson was certainly one of their best men. It irritated him that young Milstein was gumming up the works for Jackson. Milstein was a new man in the department and evidently had a few things to learn.

Sitting at his desk, where he had dealt with so many weighty academic matters, Dr. Peate chewed thoughtfully on the fifteen-cent cigar that had been given to him that morning by a textbook salesman. It was an excellent cigar, but he had been curt with the salesman. He had not liked his looks nor his intellectual air. Salesmen took up far too much of his valuable time. Dr. Peate stared glassily at the rows of books in the case above his desk, many of them sample textbooks which had been presented to him by other young salesmen whose looks he had not liked. Most of the books had numerous uncut pages. He pretended to finish what he had pretended he was doing.

"So Milstein said he was going to flunk you, did he?" he said finally.

"Yeh, that's what he said."

"Just what seems to be the trouble between you and Milstein, Jackson?"

"I don't know. I just can't seem to get that stuff through my head, Doc. It's tough. He springs tests on us all the time."

"Doesn't give you warning, eh?"

It was a practice Dr. Peate frowned on. At the beginning of each quarter, Dr. Peate handed out a complete outline of the work, indicating the dates of the examinations and how much each counted towards the final grade. He had suggested that this procedure be followed by all instructors of Freshman English, but a few, like Milstein, totally disregarded his suggestion.

Dr. Peate took the cigar from his mouth and looked at it. It had gone out. He noticed that he had slobbered a good deal. He decided to take a new approach with Jackson.

"Jackson, what is a participle?"

"Huh? Participle? You got me there."

"Don't you know what a participle is?"

"Doc, I don't see the percentage in that course. I came here instead of going to Wisconsin because they made it look good to me, see? And if I have to mess around with grades all the time—well, I just don't see the percentage."

"I think that I'll be able to straighten it out all right," Dr. Peate said reassuringly. "You've been attending Milstein's classes regularly, haven't you? Have to be careful about cuts, you know!"

"Hardly a cut. You think you can fix it up, Doc?"

"I think so. I think so. Don't worry about it." Dr. Peate turned the cigar between his fingers and decided that he ought to put in a few words about discipline. "But I want you to start hitting the ball, Jackson," he said. "Hit the ball, and learn how to study. After all, you've got to make good at keeping up with your studies. You're in college for something more than just football, you know!"

Just off-hand, Dr. Peate did not know what else Jackson was in college for. It was another thing, though, that was not worth dwelling on.

Jackson hunched his shoulders and bit down on the match between his teeth. "I do the best I can, but this course of Milstein's is tough, know what I mean? He's always putting me in a tough spot."

Dr. Peate became suddenly alert. "He is? Just how, Jackson? Just how does he put you on the spot?"

"He kids me in class, gives me the razz in front of everybody. Some day I'm going to take a poke at that kike."

"Now, now, I wouldn't advise that, Jackson. That's the wrong attitude, altogether. Next quarter I'll get you transferred to Mr. Armstrong's class. For the time being, I want you to get along with Mr. Milstein."

"Think you can fix it up, Doc?"

"I feel confident of it."

"If you don't, I'll be up the creek."

"I'll do my best. And get all those foolish ideas out of your head about doing Mr. Milstein any physical harm. We don't get any place that way, you know."

When Jackson had gone, Dr. Peate sat in his swivel chair and listened to the sound of the football player's heel-plates tapping on the tile floor of the hallway. He kept thinking about his wife. He drank a glass of water, irritably rattled some papers on his desk, and pulled at the crotch of his pants. He had told Dr. Ogilvie, the head of the English Department, not to hire Milstein in the first place. They had never had any luck with Jews, he reflected. One of them had written proletarian poems. They had got rid of him in a hurry. Another, Mr. Kauffman, they had discovered after he had gone on to Harvard, had been living with a blonde who worked as a typist for the Federal Housing Authority. They had been quite open about it. A lot of people had known. The blonde had been a good-looker, too. But in the face of both examples, Ogilvie had been a big enough fool to hire another Jew, this Milstein. It demonstrated Ogilvie's lack of sense and administrative ability well enough.

He took out his watch, which had been presented to him by the team in 1928. It had his initials engraved on it. It was a quarter to four. Milstein's afternoon class would be over very shortly. It was a special class in English for students in the College of Dentistry.

Dr. Peate opened a couple of letters that had come, trying to shake off the uneasy feeling that had settled on him. Dealing with most of the instructors, who he knew were afraid of him, was perfectly easy. With Milstein it would not be so easy. He had disliked Milstein from the first. He had to read the message in his hand over again; he had been considering how he would deal with Milstein. The situation was not without its difficulties.

The message was a routine mimeographed affair from the Office of the Chancellor, announcing the appointment of Karl Leonard Schrunck, B.S., Ph.D. (Northwestern), who was to take the place vacated by the death of Dr. Mirrilees. Dr. Mirrilees had been the head of the Physics Department. He had passed away following a boiler explosion in the basement of his home several weeks before. The mimeographed announcement did not mention the boiler explosion. Dr. Peate regarded the appointment with dissatisfaction. He felt that they should have given the job to Dr. Chambers, instead of bringing in a new man. He dropped the paper in the wastebasket and opened the other envelope.

He would confront Milstein with his unfair treatment of Jackson in the classroom. There was no possible excuse for that. He would remind him that ridicule was out of place there. He would walk down the hall and go into Milstein's office. "What's this business about Merle Jackson?" he would begin. He would be affable at first, but firm, of course. If Milstein seemed intractable, he would get nasty.

The other envelope contained a reminder that his dues at the Faculty Club were long past due. He put it in the wastebasket on top of the Schrunck communication.

After the bell had rung, he waited for a few moments for the halls to clear. He relighted his cigar, puffing with an air that suggested thought. It was a good idea for him to have the cigar. It gave a tone of authority.

Some dental students were standing in the hallway when he emerged from his office, glumly examining the bulletin board. There had been nothing new on it for weeks. Dr. Peate glanced into Milstein's classroom. It was empty. He went on down to Milstein's office.

Milstein was standing by the window, smoking a cigarette and blowing rings, when Dr. Peate entered without knocking. His face wore the look of fatigue brough on by talking to dental students for a long class period. Dr. Peate knew that Milstein was a Jew, but he did not look like a Jew. That is, he did not look like Dr. Peate's idea of what a Jew should look like. This always made him uneasy. Things like that should be sharply defined, clear-cut, easy to pigeonhole. He would have liked it better if Milstein looked like the cartoons one sometimes saw of Jews. It would have simplified matters.

"Little problem I wanted to see you about, Mr. Milstein," Dr. Peate began, removing the cigar from his mouth.

"Won't you have a chair?" Milstein asked politely. "Wonderful weather, isn't it?"

Milstein was too affable. It threw Dr. Peate off his guard for a moment.

"I believe you have a student in 101b," said Dr. Peate, declining the offer of a chair. "Merle Jackson."

"Oh, yes," Milstein said. "Very stupid young man, too. He hasn't been to class for almost two weeks now."

Things weren't going at all well. Dr. Peate chewed on his cigar. "Really?" he said. "Two weeks, eh?"

"Two weeks," Milstein said.

"Hmmm, that's not so good."

"He's very badly behaved in class, falls asleep, sits far in the back and talks to a girl who's usually with him. Altogether one of the worst students I have in all of my classes."

"Hmmm."

"What about him, Doctor?"

"Well, he was in to see me just now, and he told me that you make a practice of ridiculing him during the class hour."

"You don't say," Milstein said politely. "Well, on a couple of

157

occasions I reminded him, when he came in late, that the class met at eight, not at eight-fifteen or eight-thirty. He must be unusually sensitive. I had no idea I'd wounded his feelings. Football player, isn't he?"

"Er, yes. Now, that's what I wanted to talk to you about, Milstein. Some of these football men, like Jackson, have a rather difficult time getting through school. Long practice hours, games; Jackson's working his way through, you know; it puts a big burden on some of the boys. Now if you turn Jackson in at the six weeks as failing, it will mean that he'll be unable to finish out the season."

"Play football, you mean?"

"Exactly," Dr. Peate said, nodding.

"I hadn't thought of that."

It looked as though Milstein would be reasonable, Dr. Peate thought. Perhaps he had gotten the wrong idea about Milstein. He smiled. "I think you appreciate the situation," he went on. "I'm sure that if you don't turn him in this time, he'll snap right out of it and come through with flying colors. I can virtually promise you that. I've seen a lot of cases like this; taken a lot of them in hand myself and pulled them through in great shape."

"I've already turned in the grades," said Milstein, putting his cigarette out.

"Oh, well! There won't be any trouble about that. Just send a note over to the office; say that it was an error on the part of your reader. Very simple little matter to attend to."

Milstein was regarding him with a queer smile that Dr. Peate did not like at all.

"They won't think anything of it," Dr. Peate went on hurriedly. "Little errors like that are cropping up all the time."

"I'm sure they do," Milstein said calmly. He took a pack of cigarettes from his coat. "Will you have a cigarette, Doctor? Oh, I'm sorry; I didn't see your cigar."

"You don't consider this sort of thing questionable, I hope!" Dr. Peate said with a disarming laugh. "After all, I do feel that we have to take a lot of factors into consideration. Jackson may be no great shakes in the classroom, but he's one of the most important men on the team this year. I hope you'll give me your word that you'll send that little correction over to the office right away."

Milstein shook his head. He still wore the queer smile that Dr. Peate disliked. "I'm afraid it's utterly out of the question, Dr. Peate."

"And why is it out of the question?"

"Well, I was hired to teach English, and in my English class this Jackson is without doubt absolutely moronic. He's surly, indifferent, cocky. He hasn't demonstrated in any way that he even wants to learn anything. In simple justice, Dr. Peate, I can't give him anything but a failing grade. If he shows improvement from now on, I'll be more than happy to change his grade. But it isn't fair to ask me to pretend that I made an error. I'm afraid that grade will have to stand."

Dr. Peate was boiling. His face was red, and he could feel the large vein on his temple beating. He pressed his cigar firmly between his fingers. "I think you're making a very big mistake, Milstein," he said shortly.

"I hope not, Doctor."

Dr. Peate tried to get a grip on himself. The situation was running away from him. "I want you to sleep on this," he said. "Think it over; then let me know definitely in the morning. We don't want to make any rash, foolish decisions."

"I'm afraid that I'll have to say the same thing in the morning. I'm sorry."

"Very well, Milstein," Dr. Peate said. "Very well, if that is to be your attitude."

He walked hurriedly out of the office, tripping on the doorsill and barely avoiding falling flat on his face. He attempted to recover his dignity, but two of his students, coming out of the washroom, had observed his embarrassment. He walked on down the hall erectly, his shoulders back, his step springy. He had special arch-preservers fitted into all of his shoes.

The arch-preservers dated from his first days in the hiking club.

His anger cooled when he got his hat from his own office and started for home. It had been his intention, earlier in the day, to go over to the stadium, as he often did, to watch the boys practice. He was in no mood for it now. He would go home and take a bracing cold shower and drink a glass of carrot juice. Those things had a way of relaxing him, as well as pepping up his mind. He would get around Milstein some way. He had had to deal with situations of this sort before.

He was anxious to see if there was any word at the hotel about his wife. He hurried along the street.

Under the awning of the Whittier Hotel doorway, Dr. Peate stopped to buy an evening paper from the cripple who was there every evening. The cripple was a war veteran with a complexion the color of old oilcloth. Dr. Peate did not like to look at him, but it did not seem right to buy his paper elsewhere and then walk right by the cripple. He waited for his two cents change and went into the lobby. Like the rest of the hotel, it was plain but homelike. That was Dr. Peate's way of describing it.

The desk clerk handed him his key and a yellow envelope. The clerk had once been a student of Dr. Peate's at the University.

"Telegram for you, Dr. Peate."

"Hmmm," Dr. Peate said. "Thank you, Ronald."

In the elevator he removed his hat in deference to a heavyset, perfumed woman with a fox terrier. She talked to it all the way up to the ninth floor, where she got off. Dr. Peate got off at the eleventh floor.

He opened the telegram as soon as he was in his room. It was beginning to get dark, and he sat down in his easy chair by the window and snapped on the light.

MRS. PEATE DIED 2:35 TODAY   SHALL WE MAKE FUNERAL ARRANGEMENTS?

S. D. KITCHELL

He read it over several times. He decided that he had better go down himself; they would pile up big expenses if he wasn't there to keep an eye on them.

He undressed and took a cold shower. After drying himself, he medicated his feet with a new salve he was experimenting with. He put on his pajamas and dressing gown and went to the little kitchenette, where he poured out a brimming glass of carrot juice. Dr. Peate did not eat an evening meal.

The relief that he felt over his wife's death made the disagreement with Milstein seem utterly unimportant. He had been letting his sense of values get out of hand. Milstein was very small fry. There were lots of ways of dealing with him. He would take care of that the first thing in the morning, and then catch the noon bus to Woodlawn.

After drinking his carrot juice, he washed the glass and dried it carefully. He went in the other room and looked at himself in the mirror. He took a deep interest in his mirror-image. Taking his eyes away from it with difficulty, he went through his daily exercises and then worked the cross-word puzzle in the newspaper he had bought from the cripple. He kept thinking how silly he had been, allowing himself to get so worked up by a person like Milstein. There were lots of ways to fix him. Before turning in, he telephoned Ronald at the desk and left a call for seven in the morning.

"I hope you didn't have any bad news in your telegram, Dr. Peate," Ronald said.

"Oh no," Dr. Peate said. "No bad news."

"That's good. Plenty of heat in your room?"

"Yes, it's very comfortable.... You got that call, didn't you? Seven o'clock?"

"Yes, I have it."

"Well, good night, Ronald."

He started to hang up.

"Oh, Dr. Peate?"

"Yes?"

"I meant to ask you—how are you betting on the game next Saturday?"

"You know me. I always bet on my own boys."

"Think they're going to take it, do you?"

"I've never been so sure of anything in my life."

"What about Jackson? Fellow was telling me tonight that he's down in his grades and won't be able to play."

"I don't think there's anything to it, Ronald."

"You don't?"

"I don't think there's a thing to it. I feel absolutely confident that Jackson will play Saturday. Absolutely confident."

"I'm sure glad to hear you say that. It had me a little worried.... Well, good night, Dr. Peate."

"Good night, Ronald," Dr. Peate said.

EVERY YEAR THEY CAME OUT

THEY HAD NOT been able to get the room at the hotel that they liked, the one they always had. The room they preferred to all the others was on the fourth floor, facing the park and the boulevard. It had a little balcony on which they could sun themselves on good mornings.

It was because of Miss Cora's negligence that they had to take, instead, a dark, unpleasant room at the back. It offered nothing in the way of a view. Before they had left Nebraska, Miss Ernestine instructed Miss Cora, since Miss Ernestine was the senior sister as well as the dominant one, to write for reservations. "Write them that we want our old room, 417, the same as always," she told her early in September. Later, having some doubt in her mind about her sister's capability, Miss Ernestine asked Miss Cora if she had carried out her instructions, and Miss Cora said, "Yes, Ernestine, I'm quite positive that I wrote them." "Quite positive!" said Miss Ernestine. "Did you write to them or didn't you?" "I think I did," Miss Cora had said.

It was an unconvincing reply, and Miss Ernestine had remarked rather acidly that it was scarcely enough for her to think that she had written. What she wanted to know was: *Had* she or had she not? Well, Miss Cora had said, she was almost positive. Yes, she remembered now. She remembered sitting down one morning and writing a letter to the hotel people. Yes, it all came back to her now. She was very definite about it.

But, as it turned out, the manager of the hotel had received no

163

word at all from them. They had arrived in Los Angeles by train on the eighteenth of October, tired out from the long journey and from the berths in which neither of them had slept well, and irritable because they had not had their daily baths, only to find out, after a frightened ride with a surly and careless taxi-driver who they felt sure was bent on destroying them both, that Miss Cora had not written after all. She had not written, and there were only two rooms left.

For days Miss Ernestine had given Miss Cora no peace. Suddenly, in the middle of a sentence about something totally unrelated to their room, she would break off to say, "Cora, why in Heaven's name didn't you *tell* me you hadn't written? Certainly you should have had that much sense."

"Ernestine, please. I'm so awfully sorry. Why don't we go to another hotel?"

"I don't want to go to another hotel."

"But you're so upset. And we always come here."

"I am *not* upset. Honestly, it's getting so I can't depend upon you to do the simplest things right."

"Ernestine, if you don't like this room, why don't we pick up and go someplace else? There are lots of other hotels. I've told you I don't know how many times how sorry I am about not writing for reservations. It happened, and we can't do anything about it now."

"It's all very well to be sorry," said Miss Ernestine grimly. "But that does not alter the fact that we are in this abominable little room."

"Please, Ernestine, let's move to another hotel."

"I am certainly not going to. We've been staying in this hotel for ten years. I'm used to it here. I am certainly not going to go to all that trouble."

It was actually their eighth winter in the hotel. The hotel had been recommended to them originally by Mrs. Griffin, a friend of their mother. Mrs. Griffin was a Christian Scientist who had spent her last years in Los Angeles, in order to be close to the heart of Christian Science. She had lived there until she had died, or whatever it is that Christian Scientists do when they no longer give the appearance of having life. Mrs. Griffin had almost converted Mrs. Cuthrell, the mother of Miss Cora and Miss Ernestine, to this faith, but the daughters had remained Episcopalians. One reason they had for liking the hotel was its close proximity to their favorite Episcopal church in Los Angeles.

Every winter Miss Ernestine and Miss Cora came out to Los Angeles, sometimes in October and sometimes in November. They would stay until Spring. Then they would return to Nebraska. They were both extremely cold-blooded and liked to get back to Nebraska for the hot weather. They liked the scorching summer heat. It made them feel alive.

It was a curious phenomenon that neither of the Cuthrell sisters perspired. On the hottest days, when there were numerous deaths from heat-prostration and all who found it possible were inside their houses with all the windows closed and the curtains pulled down and electric fans blowing on cakes of ice, the Cuthrell sisters would think nothing at all of working in their flower garden under the blistering sun. They would work together in the heat, Ernestine nervously, giving directions, and Cora slowly and painstakingly. They would not perspire.

Behind the Cuthrell sisters was money, and behind them, too, importantly, were their ancestors. Their father had been a judge on the bench of the State Supreme Court. In their home in Nebraska, above the mantelpiece, across from the head that had once belonged to a deer the judge had shot, was an oil painting of the judge in his black robes. He wore a cold, stern expression. He had enjoyed wearing this expression while posing for the portrait. It was a good likeness. The Cuthrell sisters admired but secretly feared the painting of their father, for his expression in it was the same one he had affected when reprimanding the members of his family. He used the same expression, too, when handing down a decision from the bench. It was the way Miss Ernestine and Miss Cora remembered him. Although he had enjoyed wearing this expression while posing for the picture, he had not had the opportunity of enjoying it for long. He had died of a heart attack three weeks after it was completed.

Their mother had died three years before the judge's attack, and their older brother, Harvey, had been killed in the first World War in an airplane crash. He had voluntarily enlisted with the Canadians before the United States had gone in. There had seemed, at the time, no reason for his extremely hasty enlistment, but shortly after he had sailed for France, the Cuthrells had had an unwelcome visitor. She was a girl who had worked in the basement of Birnbaum's Department Store. She no longer worked there, however; they had let her out. She was pregnant. Even the Cuthrells could see that. The girl, whose name was Marjorie Jergenson, told them that the child she was going to have, in a few months, was Harvey's. The judge was furious. He had ordered her from the house. But after the judge's death, they had learned that he had given her money to go to Omaha and have the child. He had been sending her fifty dollars a month.

Miss Ernestine and Miss Cora never discussed Harvey. They would never, under any circumstances, discuss Marjorie Jergenson. If either of them ever thought of Marjorie Jergenson, they did not speak of her. They would talk about the judge, reverently and briefly, and they would talk about their mother, sadly and with nostalgia, and at considerable length; but Harvey and their younger brother, William, who had stayed in the East after a sensational two years at Princeton, and who drank heavily and had been divorced twice, were not subjects for discussion. There was still a comfortable income from the judge's estate; there was money in the bank back in Nebraska; and there was more money pinned to the inside of Miss Ernestine's corset, unpinned at night and placed cautiously beneath her pillow. Miss Ernestine and Miss Cora did not have to worry about finances.

They had many friends in Los Angeles. Quite a number of them lived in the hotel. They were people from the middlewest who spent the winter in much the same manner as Miss Cora and Miss Ernestine. In the morning there were automobile rides and in the afternoon there was bridge and in the evenings, the movies. Miss Ernestine would walk through the lobby of the hotel, large and impressive and dressed in a black dress with a bit of white lace and very dignified, with the bankroll pinned in her corset, followed by Miss Cora, slighter and with a face that some called tragic, with a small amount of money, not in her corset, but in her purse; and they would eat all of their meals in the hotel dining room and be called Miss Cuthrell by the waiters. They would walk, on sunny afternoons, on Wilshire Boulevard, looking into the shop windows and sometimes going into the shops to look and sometimes, less frequently, to buy, and on Thursdays they would take a bus to visit the Grahams in Pasadena, and on Mondays they would visit some distant relatives of their mother in Long Beach.

It was a pleasant pattern of existence for them that had been disrupted, shattered, by the new room. Eventually, they knew, the people who were in their old room, a Swiss and his wife, would leave. Then they could fit perfectly into the pattern again. But the Swiss and his wife, who were considered somewhat mysterious and aloof by many at the hotel, were staying much longer than anyone had thought. The Swiss and his wife would go in and out of the hotel at odd hours, and they struck up no friendships with the other guests. "Just when do we get our old room?" Miss Ernestine would ask the hotel manager, while Miss Cora looked the other way; and the hotel manager would tell her that the Swiss were sure to leave almost any day. They had already stayed much longer than anyone had expected.

One night matters reached a crisis. Miss Ernestine and Miss Cora were returning from Long Beach after seeing the Morrises, the distant relatives there, and on the way back they had a fierce argument. Miss Ernestine was very irritable because of a call Miss Cora had failed to make to a friend of theirs, Mrs. Partridge, as she had been told to do. It was night when they returned. A band was playing for the opening of a new market and the spotlights were sending their long beams into the sky.

In their room they took baths and Miss Ernestine unpinned the money from her corset and placed it under her pillow, talking continually while Miss Cora attempted to read. Miss Cora looked out of the window. She held the book in her lap, opened to page nine. She could see nothing but a light in a room across the court. They were right next to the elevator. That was another thing that was wrong.

It was then that they heard some people in the room next to theirs. They had never been bothered previously in this fashion. It was a man and woman, and they heard the man say something to the woman that they had not heard since they were little girls. It was an expression that they thought they would never hear again. At least they knew that it was an expression which would never be addressed directly to either of them. Miss Cora was no longer looking out of the window. Miss Ernestine was standing by the bed that let down from the wall. She was wearing an old-fashioned nightgown. They heard the man use the same expression again, and then he laughed. The woman was talking to him. Her voice was soft, but they could hear it. Then they heard a strange noise that they had never heard before, not even when they were little girls. The bed squeaked.

Miss Ernestine was quivering. "Animals!" she said.

Miss Cora was looking out of the window. She had closed her book.

"Animals!" Miss Ernestine said again. "And you! You're the one who's responsible for this!"

"Oh, Ernestine!"

"If you'd only had enough sense to write for reservations, we'd never have to put up with this. We'd be back in our old room."

"Don't listen to them. Pretend they aren't there."

"Don't listen to them! How can I help listening to them?" She stood for a moment looking at the wall as though she wished to tear it down. "I'm going to pound on that wall!" she said.

"No, Ernestine, no! You mustn't."

"I'm going to pound on that wall!"

"No, no!" Miss Cora hurriedly rose from her chair and took Miss Ernestine by the arms. "No, you mustn't, you mustn't!" she said.

They were looking at each other. Their faces were close to each other. Miss Ernestine was breathing heavily. There was a great tenseness in her arms.

"Let go of me!" she said.

"Tell me you won't do it."

"Let go of me!" Miss Ernestine commanded.

Miss Ernestine broke away. She stood I the middle of the room, glaring at her sister. Her breath came fast. "Get out!" Miss Ernestine was shouting. "Get out of this room!"

Miss Cora looked at her.

"Did you hear me?" said Miss Ernestine. She was almost screaming with rage. "Get out! Get out!"

"Ernestine," Miss Cora said pleadingly.

"Get out of this room! I never want to see you again!"

There was a knock at their door.

"Who's there?" Miss Ernestine called out.

"Bellboy, miss. Is everything all right?"

"Yes, yes, of course. What's the matter?"

"It's pretty late, miss. Would you mind lowering your voice?"

Miss Ernestine was rigid. Her jaws quivered angrily as she looked about the room. They could hear the bellboy going away from the door. They heard him go down the hall to the elevator and then the sound of the elevator door opening and closing.

"Never in all my life!" said Miss Ernestine. "I will not stay under this roof another night. Come on, Cora, don't just stand there! Help me get packed. We're getting out right now."

"Ernestine—"

"Help me get packed!"

They paid the bill in full at the desk. Miss Ernestine had counted out the correct amount before pinning the roll back into her corset. They took a cab to a hotel where Miss Williamson, a friend of theirs, lived. It was a hotel for women guests only. In the morning they slept late and in the afternoon they went for an automobile ride with Miss Williamson and her brother, a man who sold raw motion picture film. They thought they would like it very well in the new hotel. They did not talk about their quarrel, and they did not talk about the man and woman they had heard in the other hotel the night before.

In the lobby of the new hotel there were many women with dogs on leashes. Their room was airy and bright and looked out on a quiet street. Miss Ernestine said that she thought it was one of the nicest rooms they had ever had anywhere. She said she thought they might as well plan to come back to it the following year. She asked Miss Cora what she though of the idea, and Miss Cora said yes, she thought that that would be nice to do. Miss Cora said she would just as soon do that as anything else.

A Chronological Checklist of
Weldon Kees's Published Short Stories

COMPILED BY DANA GIOIA

AND BARBARA C. WEBBER

1934

Saturday Rain (*Prairie Schooner*, Fall)

1935

Frog in the Pool (*Prairie Schooner*, Spring)

Summer Morning Early (*Prairie Schooner*, Summer)

End of a Season (*The New Day*, July)

Escape in Autumn (*Windsor Quarterly*, Winter)

1936

This is Home (*Manuscript*, May-June)

Letter from Maine (*Prairie Schooner*, Summer)

Three Pretty Nifty Green Suits (*Prairie Schooner*, Winter)

Noon (*Manuscript*, November-December)

A Day's Query (*Horizon* [New York], November-December)

1937

A Man to Help (*Horizon* [New York], January-February)

A Walk Home (*Frontier & Midland*, Spring)

The Library: Four Sketches (*Direction* 1937):

I. Back Room and Front Desk
II. Homage
III. All the Way There
IV. Miss Van Wie, Miss Quade, Miss Spangenburg

Like a New Man (*Prairie Schooner,* Summer)

Midwestern University: Evening
(*The Literary Arts,* October-November)

Mrs. Lutz (*Prairie Schooner,* Winter)

Gents 50¢ / Ladies 25¢ (*Hinterland,* I)

1938

Four Stories (*Rocky Mountain Review,* Fall):

Zuni Street Evenings
To the Traveler on the Heights Comes Faintly
Big Improvement
Two Young Men Wearing Hard Straw Hats
and Summer Wash Suits

So Cold Outside (*Prairie Schooner,* Winter)

The Sign Painters (*Hinterland,* II)

Downward and Away (*Hinterland,* No. 10)

1939

Everybody Wins (*University Review,* Spring)

Applause (*Prairie Schooner,* Summer)

These People (*Fantasy,* No. 2)

God Watches Over You, Mrs. Rambaugh (*Hinterland,* No. 13)

I Should Worry (*New Directions* 1939)

DATE DUE

Fecha Para Retorn